SCOOTER BOYS

by Gareth Brown

© Gareth Brown 1996
This edition copyright © 1996 Omnibus Press (5th Edition)
(Omnibus Press is a Division of Book Sales Limited)

ISBN 0-7119-6159-X
Order No.OP47859

Written and compiled by Gareth Brown. Cover photo of Oasis reproduced courtesy of Jill Furmanovsky, Noel Gallagher & Ignition. Cover photo of Steve from OCS by Gareth Brown. Cover photo of Paul Weller courtesy of *Scootering* magazine. Page 7 photo of Paul Weller courtesy of Laurence Watson. Group photo of OCS courtesy of Martyn Greenacre & MCA Records. Archive photographic material: Gareth Brown, *Scootering* Magazine, Steven Stratton & Andrew Campbell. Additional editorial contributions: Mark Taylor & Martin Round (Sticky). Artist liaison: Nikki Legg.

Exclusive Distributors
Book Sales Limited, 8/9 Frith Street, London W1V 5TZ, UK.
Music Sales Corporation, 257 Park Avenue South, New York, NY 10010, USA.
Music Sales Pty Limited, 120 Rothschild Avenue, Rosebery, NSW 2018, Australia.
To the Music Trade only
Music Sales Limited, 8/9 Frith Street, London W1V 5TZ, UK.

Printed in the United Kingdom by Staples Printers, Rochester, Kent.

A catalogue record for this book is available from the British Library.

Visit Omnibus Press at http://www.musicsales.co.uk

'It was a sweltering hot Saturday afternoon in the summer of '65; Dad was driving us home in our two-tone grey/green Vauxhall Wyvern after a family trip to London. I was asleep on the back seat with my sister, when, as we passed through Ilford, I was suddenly awoken by my parents' incredulous exclamations of amusement. Coming towards us was a shining silver scooter adorned with an abundance of chromed mirrors and lights. Its helmetless rider hidden behind his sunglasses, it just purred past .

Coupled with an infatuation for Sandie Shaw, which I developed in the second half of the Sixties, my impressionable young mind had subconsciously ensured that in later years this era would influence me greatly ... but I had no idea then to just what extent.'

Gareth Brown

The Postmodern Condition?

The cult of scootering has been an organic entity both musically and visually since it's humble beginnings. It has constantly embraced new ideologies and styles, sub divided where necessary to accommodate conflicting identities and - peaks apart - enjoyed a constant degree of modest self perpetuation since the 1960s. Modest self perpetuation was a definite understatement in Britain by 1995 however, as that year saw yet another peak hove clearly into view and another generation adopt and adapt aspects of Mod imagery for themselves.

At that time, resurging retrospective British music-lead Modernism, too, was developing and becoming every bit as prolific as it had been during the late Seventies and early Eighties. This was not because of Sixties revivalism though (although facets of this helped), but because anew breed of British beat band was coming to prominence and in many instance, openly extolling the virtue of the scooter.

The most noted of these are pictured in this publication and their music discussed in the closing section. These artists only represent a part of the whole however - the Nineties epoch of New Modernist culture - and as such, have had the editorial space which they have ben allotted proportioned accordingly. So if you have only picked this book up because it contains photos of Paul Weller, Oasis and Steve of OCS and subsequently expect it to be solely about them, I suggest you put it down again.

The main reason the aforementioned were asked to be included in this book (something to which they all readily agreed), is - from a scootering perspective - far more poignant than that of their music. You see each pictured, actually owns and rides the scooter they have been photographed astride. What is more, their scoots are more than mere record company props.

This is because in each instance, a passion for the scooter has preceded personal fame. In the case of

Oasis, this is highlighted by the following extract from Paolo Hewitt's interview with them as published in SELECT magazine, issue No.71, May 1996:

'Noel comes up from the back of the coach and passes Guigsy a book on scooters and a large toy scooter he's bought that morning. . . Scooters are a big thing with this band. Liam has a 1954 Vespa at home and Guigsy went on scooter runs when he was 16. Last year on holiday, Noel bought each band member a scooter. "I'm going to get a flight case made and take it on the next tour" reckons Noel. (Liam) "What about mine?"'

The scooter which Noel bought his fellow band members back from Italy, are Italijets. Although these are not the archetypical Vespas and Lambrettas associated with on-going traditional scooter culture (as explained further on in this book), they do still hail from Italy and bring to the fore a facet of New Modernism that - until relatively recently - would never have been entertained. For according to Chris, an active 'New Mod' from Essex, many Nineties Mods are buying machinery other than the accepted makes for reasons of cost and availability (although they all profess a preference for the previously mentioned mainstream marques).

Paul Weller - who has been synonymous with Modernism since the revivalist days of the Eighties - has been an avid Italian motor scooter owner since the Seventies. Currently owning a pristine Lambretta SX 200, Paul was responsible for selling Steve from OCS his first scooter in 1990. Unfortunately this was promptly stolen, but the seeds had been sewn and Steve has owned and ridden several scoots ever since - attending several rallies nationwide.

But for all the above to become interested in the scooter scene, first there had to be a one. In the Sixties this was dominated by the original Mods, in the early Seventies by the original Skinheads and in the Eighties by the inaugurally labelled Scooter Boy (latterly known as Scooterist) movement, which is still going strong today.

Each of these fractions are commented on chronologically as this book unfolds. It is not essential to read the following in any give order however, as this text has been structured in such a way as to enable the most interesting areas of scootering social history for a particular reader to be read through first (although it is hoped you will eventually digest it all). For instance, the birth of British teenage consumerism begins on page 15; Sixties Modernism on page 19; Scooter Boys on page 53 and Britpop on page 126. To start with though, we look at the solid foundations of all the aforementioned movements: the evolution of the motorised scooter. . .

Paul Weller at home on his 1967 Lambretta SX 200, with his son Nathan (up front) and Nathan's play pal.

Sowing the Seeds

Absolute Beginnings

Motorised machines that can be referred to as motor scooters have been around for a lot longer than many people may think. Arguably the first such machine was the Hildebrand And Wolfmueller, which was produced as early as 1894 both in Munich and in France. Its relatively short yet reasonably successful production run came to an end in 1896. Powered by a twin cylinder four-stroke motor, this two wheeled machine featuring many characteristics associated with the scooter was capable of speeds of 24mph (38kph). Also featuring a larger than usual front wheel, the Hildebrand And Wolfmueller was still a far cry from the style of scooter we know today.

Many other machines appeared over the next twenty years which can be considered as early motor scooters, such as the American Autoped of 1916 which was produced under license both in the United Kingdom and Germany. It wasn't until the ABC Skootamobile produced by the Sopwith Aviation Co Ltd came along in 1919 though that the recognisable format for the scooter of the future was established. This ABC Skootamobile had two equal-sized small wheels, a clear central section featuring floor boards, and a single saddle seat with the engine mounted behind it.

World War Two saw another addition to the scooter family courtesy of the Welbike folding scooter. Dropped in pods by parachute, once unfolded, these collapsible machines were used by Allied paratroopers as 'instant transport' when landing in occupied Europe. It was as a direct result of the Second World War that the most popular and well known scooter of all time came into existence.

Having been destroyed by the United States Airforce in a bombing raid, the Italian aircraft manufacturing plant of Piaggio and Co at Pontedera decided in 1945 that they needed to start producing something new in order to help them pick up the pieces. Dr Enrico Piaggio

An ABC Skootamobile

A British '50's DKR Dove

came up with the idea of a small two-wheeled machine, and handed the project over to one of the factory's leading engineers - Corradino d'Ascanio.

Trained as an aviation engineer, Corradino had only a limited knowledge of the two-wheeled field, but through the application of approved engineering stan-dards, he came up with what was to become one of Italy's biggest post-war engineering and marketing success stories.

Of the first machines, only one hundred or so were built, but when the final design emerged and was officially launched at the Turin show in 1946, production began in earnest. Corradino d'Ascanio named this new machine the Wasp, which in Italian is Vespa ...

Within the first ten years of production, Piaggio had sold over one million of their new Vespa motor scooters; which they followed up with a further million over the next five years. By that time Piaggio had a number of competitors - the most importance of which was the Innocenti company based in Milan in northern Italy. Innocenti were noted for their production of steel tubing and heavy engineering. They exported steel rolling machines to South America, and had a good working relationship with the coachbuilding firm of Pininfarina who were famous for their designs in the car world. This helped Innocenti greatly when they started producing their own version of the motor scooter in 1947. These machines were named after the suburb of Milan in which they were made; Lambrate. Thus the Lambretta had been born.

Despite their constructional differences (the Vespa having a pressed steel frame and the Lambretta's being made out of tubular steel), these two scooters were to come to virtually corner the entire British scooter market. Before they could do this though, they had a battle on their hands.

Scootermania - Mobility for the Masses.

When scootermania swept across Europe in the Fifties and Sixties, it found an assortment of Anglo-Allies. Many manufacturers involved with the then-thriving British motor-cycle industry had started to produce

A 1959 Moto Rumi Tipo Sport

A 1958 Lambretta Li 150 series 1

their own types of scooter. With some using bought-in Villiers engines, these British scooters came from companies such as Triumph, BSA, Sunbeam, DKR, and James - just to name a few.

The Germans and French started producing motor scooters around this time too, as did two other Italian companies - Ducati and Capri. Despite a hard-fought commercial fight, none of these scooters ever really took off. Admittedly these machines were designed primarily with function rather than form in mind, but they all seemed to lack one very important ingredient - aesthetic appeal.

The Vespa and the Lambretta were seen as the personification of the purist Italian styling. Their classic lines became they key to their success throughout the continent, with Vespa having the definite edge everywhere except in Britain.

But why this sudden international interest in scooters? The reasons seem to be two-fold:

Firstly, and probably most importantly, was the increased desire for individual mobility in the years immediately following the Second World War; and the second was the creation of the scooter commuter consumer market. The proof that this new market had been created was clear. If the initial success of the scooter could only be attributed merely to the requirement for transport, once public transport, car and motor-cycle production, and road renovation resumed, the scooter would have faced dautingly tough competition. As it was, the motor scooter went from strength to strength, until it reached its full market potential in the mid Sixties.

With the most popular of these machines featuring smallish capacity single cylinder two-stroke engines (usually 125 or 150cc as seen on the Vespa and Lambretta), they were cheap to run, easy to maintain, instantly affordable, and - quite simply - fun to ride. They offered a degree of freedom and personal movement at a very small cost - both in terms of capital outlay and running expenses - hitherto unheard of or experienced by the less affluent citizens of Europe, and - coupled with the undeniable Italian panache - as such were virtually guaranteed complete commercial success!

An early 1950's Vespas

Tearaway Teds

The Fifties saw the creation of another crucially important new British consumer market where there previously had been none - the teenager. Up until then, adolescents can be said to have moved straight from childhood to being a young adult without an intervening period of identity. All this was to change, and with dramatic and long-lasting results. As many school leavers were gaining good paying employment, the demand grew for relatively frivolous fashionable items which could absorb the surplus cash left in their pockets after they had paid their usually nominal keep.

Right across the class spectrum young people had been dressed as - and expected to behave as - slightly smaller versions of their parents, but now the concept of the teenager was emerging with a new and very distinct identity. These new teenager fashion followers came primarily from the lower classes; as the upper middle and upper classes preserved a 'hold' over their offpring much longer.

Teenagers expressed their boredom and dissatisfaction with the clothes and music of their parents generation and started to look to the USA for inspiration. To their great delight they found many influences, including early Rock 'N Roll. Not only was this music lively, exciting and completely new, but it had an added attraction; the collective and vehement disapproval of their parents - which, of course, made it all the more seductive. Rock 'N Roll's meteoric rise in popularity was inevitable. Its widespread appeal was seen by adults and the totally adult- orientated media as reaching epidemic proportions among young people throughout the Western world.

The style of dress adopted by these early followers of British teenage fashion also became firmly fixed in the new Rock 'N Roll movement - but took their influences from the Edwardian period - almost as a pastiche of current upper class dress. The men wore tight 'drain pipe' trousers, longer than usual jackets with trimmed collars and cuffs (called drape coats because of their cut), elaborate waistcoats and string ties, expensive pointed-toed shoes or boots, grew side burns and greased back their hair into elaborate quiffs. This look originated completely in the UK, but the girls on the other hand, wore the American style of full circular calf-length skirts, with their hair either up in a 'beehive' style, or a long 'pony tail sprouting from their crown. These fashion conscious teenagers were graced - courtesy of the press - with the collective name 'Teddy Boys, Teddy Girls' or simply 'Teds'. Such nick-names were derived, fairly obviously, from the abbreviations of Edward ... or Edwardian.

The Teddy Boy cult seems overly gaudy nowadays, and in many ways gauche; but it was the first true teenage cult and they needed to stand out from the crowd, and to advertise the arrival of the new face of adolescence. To the eyes of the general public however, this was seen as the birth of juvenile delinquency.

The mid Fifties saw catalysts such as the film Rock Around The Clock open in Britain. The national papers were full of sensational stories about hoards of Teds (the name was used initially as a derogatory term) wielding cut-throat razors, slashing and smashing up cinemas, and generally going on the rampage both during and after the film. Although a degree of civil unrest did take place, in many cases the worst that really happened was that the film inspired dancing and jiving in the various cinema aisles. Society was shocked and outraged. Spontaneity was frowned on. The odd incident of destructive disorder which did break out can be attributed more to the bottled-up frustrations and resentments felt by these teenagers towards their elders, rather than a total disregard for people and property. The same motivation and violence was to rear its head again twenty years later in the Punk movement of the Seventies, and for broadly similar reasons - though the economic and employment situations were by then very different.

Given that this is a book about Scooterists, the history of the Teds might not seem immediately relevant - but there are two very important similarities; which no other youth cultures share. Firstly, both styles were created purely in the UK and did not 'ape' foreign - or especially, American styles; with foreign influences being adopted later. Teds and Mods were uniquely British fashions, as was Punk ... but Teds and Mods, unlike Punks, adopted two-wheeled transport, and crucially, made no stylistic concessions at all to the practicalities which any sort of bike transport ought to demand. Rockers, greasers, Hells Angels, and bikers all owed part or all of their appearance to the dictates of

Scooter Boys

their mode of transport; the rocker uniform came out of motorcycling practicalities almost completely: not so Teds and Mods - whose emergence, despite the very different social conditions, had much in common.

After only three years, teenage fashions left the Teds behind and moved to pastures new, as style began to influence fashion by adding a degree of subtlety - increasing its acceptability without compromising its credibility.

Butlins, Filey 1955

The Swinging Sixties

As the Sixties dawned, America's influence on style began to wane. For this, the start of what in later years would be known as the 'Swinging Sixties' brought with it - in more ways than one - a whole new era. In time, the Sixties would introduce bisexual and asexual clothing styles, a degree of sexual freedom, a new and broader drug culture, and two independent but opposing teenage factions. The disagreements between these two groups would manifest in media-hyped altercations at coastal resorts around the country. But first, their differences would become all too apparent ...

Modamorphasis

Style conscious young Britons came closer to home for their fashionable inspiration in the opening years of the Sixties, as the 'Continental Look' came into vogue. French and Italian clothes were adopted, adapted, and Anglicised - until they offered the perfect alternative for those with a thirst for both change and individuality.

The then-thriving coffee bar culture became the forum via which these new dress codes spread - first seen in the late Fifties, on the backs of the 'Coffee Bar Cats'. These fashions consisted of single or double-breasted jackets - one or two buttoned, with thin-lapels and a short ventless box back (known as bum-freezers); tapered tight trousers, winkle-picker and later chisel-toed cuban-heeled boots or shoes, thin ties, and 'College Boy' hair cuts.

The followers of this new direction in teenage fashion came largely from the middle classes - in particular the affluent Jewish communities of London suburbia. With many of their families being in the tailoring trade, 'customised' clothing was not a problem. But just owning the clothes was not enough. They had to be aired at all the right places - in order to do this, these trendy teenagers needed to be mobile. Cars were too expensive, and motor-cycles too dirty. The scooter, however, offered the perfect alternative - cheap to run, clean, and - importantly - it added to the all important continental image.

These young peacocks initially called themselves 'Individualists', or 'Stylists'. But the name which was to stick was derived from their choice of music. In contrast to the predominantly middle-class 'Beatniks' who had surfaced in the Fifties and had a taste for Traditional Jazz, these new Stylists preferred listening to something more in keeping with their fast forward image. Modern Jazz provided the perfect answer. This musical predilection resulted in them being called 'Modernists', which was later abbreviated to 'Mods' and thus 'Modernism' was born.

March of the Mods

Over the ensuing years, the Mod movement went from strength to strength as it found a new breeding ground at street level in the youth of the working classes. By 1964 it was truly established as an independent and dynamic movement. It was wholly self governing, self motivating, exciting, and ever changing. Its emphasis was still on style and originality, but its fashions and music had moved on from those of its mentors in the late Fifties.

Along with the 'zoot' suits, which now incorporated single breasted three-buttoned and vented jackets, and fourteen inch- bottomed hipster trousers, there was a more casual look attached to Modernism. This consisted of items such as Fred Perry collared sports shirts and jumpers, coloured cycling shirts, Levi jeans, Sta-press trousers, and an assortment of lightweight jackets featuring elasticated collars and cuffs.

Acceptable Mod footwear ranged from bowling shoes to brogues, from baseball boots to loafers, and from Chelsea Boots to Hush Puppies or desert boots (as they became known). These soft-soled, square-toed, ankle-high suede boots enjoyed popularity throughout the Mod years.

Although fewer in numbers than their male counterparts, the female element of Mod was just as important. For it was they who introduced the previously mentioned bisexual clothing and broke away from the rigorous restraints of feminine fashions. The college campus wispy waist and pretty-pretty look left over from the Fifties was replaced by the seemingly shapeless shift dress school of style now associated with the middle Sixties.

Their hair was worn short - like the boys, or in a 'Cleopatra' bob, while their faces were whited out. The eyes were darkened by liberally applying layers of Khol - a blackening agent imported from India, and false eye lashes were added to contrast with their dramatically thinned out eye brows.

Clumpy strapped granny shoes with thick inch-high heels, modified patent tap dance shoes, and suede Hush Puppies, ski pants, 'A' line skirts, and the same casual garments as worn by the boys completed their ensemble. These 'Modettes' as they became known, seemed to concentrate more on looking smart than feminine. The onus on looking pretty had seemed to switch to the boys.

For both sexes, the most recognisable garment of Modernism came as a direct result of their mode of transport: The scooter, which had to be either a Lambretta, or a Vespa. In order to protect their expensive and all important clothes from the elements, and keep warm when riding, most Mods opted to wear large ex American army olive green fish tale Parkas - the hoods occasionally trimmed with fur. These coats became synonymous with the Mod image.

By now, the scooter was of paramount importance to the projection of Modernism, and in many cases was personalised accordingly. This customising included the addition of many extra lights and mirrors, racks and back rests, whip aerials and chromed panels, and was first introduced by Eddie Grimstead's - a scooter dealer based in East London. Later the trend was completely reversed, resulting in scooters being stripped and cut down, almost to their bare frames.

Modern Music Makers.

Musically, too, the Mods were constantly moving on. Their search for new sounds had taken them from Modern Jazz, to American Rhythm and Blues - performed by artists like Rufus Thomas and Jimmy Reed, through to British Beat, and the new strain of Soul. British Beat was closely based on R&B, and came from bands like; The

Rolling Stones, The Yardbirds, The Kinks, The Who, and The Small Faces.

Soul music on the other hand, although sharing some of R&B's roots, owed more to the influence of American black gospel singing. Arguably originated by the late great Sam Cooke - a favourite in the Fifties with the Coffee Bar Cats, Soul provided something completely different. Unlike the big name beat bands - who each had their own distinctive sounds, the musical signature of Soul came from its recording labels such as Stax, Tamla Motown and Atlantic. To the discerning ear, these were easily distinguishable, and each had its devotees.

It was these musical tastes which finally high-lighted the Mods as being a separate teenage entity. Now clearly definable, the Modernist movement found its main adversary ...

Rising Rockers

The true Teddy Boys started to disappear as a direct result of massed commercialism towards the second half of the Fifties. However, many of its influences remained, and broke away into splinter groups. Those obsessed with style and fashion, eventually lead to the door of Modernism, where they bowed out, letting a new generation take over, while those with a passion for the motor-cycle, consolidated and continued. They reinforced their ranks, and eventually became the 'Rockers'.

Unlike those pursuing fashion, who congregated in the trendy bars of areas like London's West End, the domain of these motor-cyclists were the cafes of the arterials which weaved a web of roads across Britain in the pre-motorway days.

During the day, these establishments hosted holiday makers, tourists and - mostly, lorry drivers. But come the night, and they entered a whole new world. Their forecourts would look more like a motorbike show room, with virtually every make and model of the then thriving British motorcycle industry being more than adequately represented.

Where possible, their bikes would be modified until they resembled replicas of the era's road racers. This style became known as the Cafe Racer; its riders earned the title of Ton-up Boys. By the early Sixties, they had become known as 'Rockers' - unerring devotees of Fifties Rock and Roll. With many of them no longer teenagers, R&R represented their youth - where it all began. They weren't prepared to let this influence go. But to the much younger youths, the members of the Mod persuasion, they were seen as old fashioned in the extreme. Also, neither group could tolerate the others choice of transport.

The Mods' image was a continuation of fashion, the scooter an addition - albeit an important one. The Rocker's image on the other hand was born out of practicality, and the centre point of their sub-culture was the bike. Because of this their clothing - their uniform - had to be suitable for riding; tight fitting steel-blue denim or black leather jeans tucked into calf-height bike boots, with an inch or two of long white sock just showing over their top, cotton T- shirts, lumberjack or denim shirts (depending on the weather), and the all important black leather jacket. An assortment of leather caps, like those worn by Marlon Brando and his compatriots in the film The Wild Ones, along with decorative deigns in metal studs and chains on the backs of their jackets completed the look. The basic Rocker uniform was made up quite simply of items that were warm and safe, but the Rocker style truly arrived once the element of personalisation - the badges, the studs, the chains, the painted names and symbols - were added.

Mods and Rockers

Both the Mods and the Rockers now had a clearly defined and very different identity and ideology. There was more than just a generation gap separating them. They were vehemently opposed to one another, and it showed. The Mods would in time win the press propaganda war, but it would be the Rockers who'd stand the test of time - through rejuvenation and persistance.

Because of their cultural differences, the Mods and Rockers seldom came into contact with each other. This was more by luck than judgement, as to pursue their chosen life styles necessitated visiting different venues. But when a confrontation did occur, all and sundry sat up and took notice.

The Great British working class tradition of migrating to costal resorts over Bank Holiday weekends was not wasted on the Mods and Rockers. They would saddle up their steeds, along with hundreds of contemporaries, and set off for their chosen ports of call. It was a foregone conclusion that both faction's destinations would eventually prove to be one and the same.

The Weekend Wild Ones

Easter Bank Holiday, March, 1964 - Clacton Essex

The Daily Mirror reported over breakfast on the morning of Monday March 30th 1964:

'SCOOTER GANGS 'BEAT UP' CLACTON'
'The Wild Ones invaded a seaside town yesterday, 1,000 fighting, drinking, roaring, rampaging teenagers on scooters and motor- cycles. By last night, after a day of riots and battles with police, ninety-seven of them had been arrested.'

Whitsun Bank Holiday, May, 1964, Margate & Brighton

On Tuesday May 19th 1964, the Daily Sketch added to the nation's outrage by reporting:

'STABBING, STONING, DECKCHAIR BATTLES'
'The Wild Ones of Whitsun went even wilder yesterday with two beach stabbings, attacks on police and violent clashes between "Mods" and "Rockers". Holidaymakers cowered in their deckchairs as the rampaging spread from Margate to other south coast resorts - especially Brighton. The stabbings happened at Margate.'

After the August Bank Holiday of 1964, the national papers carried stories of disturbances at Hastings, Brighton, and Great Yarmouth, but none of these mentioned any head-on confrontations between the Mods and Rockers. As these clashes ceased, so did there newsworthiness, and the press went looking for a new moral outrage.

Times They Are A-Changin'

By the end of the Sixties, the Modernist had practically disappeared. Like the Teddy Boys of the Fifties, Mod fragmented in to two new camps. Its fanatical followers of fashion and liberal users of drugs (usually uppers like 'French Blues, 'Purple Hearts' and 'Black Bombers'), had moved on to the more flambouyant psychedelia - and harder drugs - in particularly the mind-warping LSD. They merged with the 'children' of the Flower Power era - the Hippie movement. Those who preferred a rougher street-level style, took a different path. Through an adaptation of the smart side of Mod which became known as the 'Suede Head' look, they evolved in to one of the most violence-orientated groups to emerge in post war Britain - the 'Skinheads'.

The press now found their new bad boys, and wasted no time in reporting on the violent clashes between the Skinheads and Greasers (as the majority of the next-generation rockers had become in the early Seventies) at Southend - again over Bank Holiday weekends. The Skinheads, who were quite prolific in the early Seventies, handed down a legacy to the up-and-coming and as-ever impressionable teenagers of that decade - the 'Boot Boys', the soccer hooligans, and the Doctor Martin boot.

These influences remained throughout the 'Glam Rock' years of the early-to-mid Seventies, and helped keep a nation of shop keepers on their toes until 'Punk' came along in 1976, and really shook things up.

From Punk to Paisley

This Was The Modern World!

The revolutionary Punk Rock explosion of the mid Seventies acted as a purifying tonic, cleansing the popular music scene of its stale commercialism - which had culminated in the likes of The Bay City Rollers, The Rubettes, and Paper Lace. Punk also brought the greatly-hyped demi-gods of music such as Rod Stewart and David Bowie down to earth with a bang.

Punks' reign, however, was to be a relatively short one. It began decomposing due to the inevitable commercial exploitation, which diluted its effect and fury. After only two real years of Punk, 1978 saw the resurgence of Disco music - but in a slightly different and arguably more palatable format, alongside commercially produced Punk and New Wave, which was purile and bland.

It was during this troubled time of turmoil, left by Punks' aftermath, that an almost forgotten fashion started to reappear on our streets - over a decade since its demise. Unknowingly, fashion and music at street level started to return to its most successful era for inspiration - the Sixties, and 'Modernism' was reborn.

Revival of the Fittest

Once things took off, it didn't take long before garments fashionable among Mods in the Sixties started to enjoy a comeback: small-collared shirts, narrow-leg trousers and jeans, Stay-Press trousers, Ben Sherman button-down collared shirts, Fred Perry T-shirts and jumpers, square-toed Frank Wright loafers, Gibson brogues and suede ankle-high desert boots - they all enjoyed a revived popularity. A universal uniform was re- born.

The Jam, a rock group spawned from Punk, contributed to these revived dress codes in no uncertain manner - as the cover of their first album 'In The City' clearly shows. In fact, the Jam were to play quite an important role in this new Mod movement, but more about that later.

Whereas many youngsters were starting to dress the part, this was mostly simply because it was 'today's fashion' - but those who had actually gone out with the sole intention of adopting the Mod image were few and far between. Many of these revivalists weren't even aware of the growth in this area, and thought themselves to be virtually unique. But this idealistic naivety was not to last.

I first became involved in the summer of '78. Being a sixteen year old who'd just left school, and clearly remembering Punk's heyday (although not directly part of it), the trend of disco music and its accompanying pegged trousers, tweed jackets, and soft Pod shoes had a limited appeal. So it was with great enthusiasm that a group of contemporaries and I acquired some Sixties suits, a selection of Sixties records, and, for the princely sum of £3, an American army-issue parka. I will also forever remember the purchase of my first scooter - a Vespa, which arrived on the back of an open truck looking very sorry for itself.

My perception of the ever-growing Mod movement was one of eager anticipation. I knew it would get bigger. I felt as though I was looking down upon a map of Britain. Wherever I envisaged a new Mod to be emerging, I would imagine a tiny red dot. I pictured these red dots to be swelling and spreading, like drips of wet ink. I dreamt that the Mod revival would reach such proportions that the whole map would be one large all-covering ink spot. Although this situation was only my personal fantasy, the Mod movement did become very big indeed, and in turn could no longer be ignored by the media.

The first national notification to the unenlightened of this growing trend in Modernism, came from the music press. They proclaimed this as the movement to end all movements, carried interviews with Ian Page - the lead singer of Secret Affair, an up-and-coming Mod band, profiled Paul Weller of The Jam, and Pete Townshend of The Who, and generally oozed with Mod enthusiasm wherever they could. It's a pity that six months later they had, of course, changed their collective minds, and gone looking, inevitably, for The Next Big Thing ...

You Need Wheels.

In these embryonic stages of the Mod revival, cheap scooters were readily available. Virtually everybody knew some old boy who had one tucked away in his shed, where it had been dumped somewhat unceremoniously at the end of the last decade. These machines (more often than not Series Three Lambretta Li 150cc scooters) could be picked up for a song; anything over £40 was considered to be excessive!

This was a far cry from the days to come, when unless you moved the decimal point one place to the right, you'd get nothing worth having at all! Still, this was the tail end of the Seventies, when as far as most were concerned, scooters were antiquated and weren't worth their weight in scrap. So if a youth offered good hard cash for something the owners thought they'd have to pay to have taken away, an amicable arrangement was agreed on instantly.

Although slightly tatty, these scooters could normally be coaxed back into life with the minimum of attention. They almost seemed relieved to once again feel the sticky texture of tarmac beneath their tiny rubber tyres. Very few scooter dealers were in existence at that time, but those who were did a roaring trade. Not necessarily by selling the new Vespas which were available, but by providing all the additional and highly essential extras that were needed to transform any scooter from being a basic machine into a mobile Mod masterpiece. Rows of spot lamps, two foot-long mirror stems (with at least two mirrors along their chromed length), tinted or coloured perspex flyscreens, front and back racks, Florida bars, crash bars, back rests, whip aerials, handle bar tassels, chrome horns, Union Jack seat covers, and chequered mud flaps which trailed on the road ... all were standard Mod equipment.

The latest news from Piaggio (the manufacturers of the Vespa) around this time, was the 'P' range Vespa. These met with a fair amount of opposition from the purist Mods, as they were seen to be too different from their predecessors, the Rally 200 and the Super 150, which still closely resembled the scooters of the Sixties. Although these new machines, too, were unmistakably Vespas, they were a bit too modern with their flashing

A new generation Modette

indicators and squarer panels (or bubbles) to be readily accepted. However, time mellowed the resistance to change and by the mid Eighties, these were the most popular scooters on the market.

Who's Quadropheniac?

Modernism - which had been enjoying a constant climb, received a number of shots in the arm in 1979, which sent its popularity soaring. Firstly from the good old BBC, who on its then regular early evening current affairs programme Nationwide, carried an in-depth article about the Mod resurgence. Second was the Sunday Observer, who virtually dedicated the whole of one week's colour supplement to Modernism, and lastly but definitely not least, the release of The Who's film - Quadrophenia.

Quadrophenia was originally an album released by The Who, dedicated to all their Mod followers from the Sixties, by way of saying thank you. But it was turned into a film by the group's own production company, and centred around a Mod called Jimmy from Shepherds Bush in London, and his adolescent problems. With the highlight being a massive re-enactment of a Mods and Rockers clash in Brighton during the riots of 1964 it was a ray of sunlight to this new school of Modernism.

Starring the young and unknown Phil Daniels as Jimmy, Sting (lead singer with The Police), Toyah Wilcox (a singer in her own right and ex-punk heroine), Leslie Ash (who as well as furthering her acting career became a competent compere for Channel 4's pop programme The Tube), and Michael Elphick (a greatly respected 'straight' actor, whose TV character Boon became popular in the Eighties), Quadrophenia was both a commercial success and a true cult film.

When I first went to see Quadrophenia - with a fellow Mod revivalist and a blonde-haired young Modette - all dressed in our Sixties finery and Parkas, we got the strangest looks from the rest of the audience as we filtered into the cinema. But on the way out, well that was a different story ... Never before, and never since have I felt so elated. The audience's recognition of myself and my friends as Mods was fantastic!

The Sound of the Suburbs

Musically, a lot of interesting things were happening around this time. The main music listened to by the revivalist was Sixties R&B from bands like The Who (particularly - of course - their 1965 rendition of My Generation), The Rolling Stones, The Yardbirds, The Small Faces, and The Kinks - along with a wide spectrum of Sixties Soul. All these styles of music were readily available by now, via numerous nostalgic compilation albums, re- pressings and a vibrant second-hand market.

One song from the Sixties even managed to creep back into the Top Twenty for the third time since its original release: Green Onions by Booker T and the MGs. This song's renewed popularity can be directly attributed to its inclusion on the sound track of Quadrophenia. When it was played on Top Of The Pops, it was accompanied by the female dance troupe Legs And Co, who wore black and white chequered plastic mini dresses.

There was also a new strain of music being closely linked to this new Mod movement, which had three very important roles to play: Firstly, it updated the movement - giving it an identity more in keeping with its new found era. Secondly it added another string to the bow of acceptable sounds, thus creating interest in the movement from a wider audience. And thirdly, it catered for those who had come across from the ranks of Punk - so helping to ease the radical changes in acceptability which faced them - as this new music contained an air of rebellion reminiscent of Punk. Many of these new bands were making it into the lime-light.

The Jam, who by now were professing themselves to be influenced by Mod, were enjoying regular success. An old standard, Poison Ivy, which had been covered and re-released by a group called The Lambrettas had reached the charts, and Secret Affair had two hits on their hands with Time For Action, and Let Your Heart Dance. This band, with both of these songs, first came to prominence on a limited edition compilation album of up and coming young Mod groups entitled Mods Mayday. This was recorded live at the Bridge House, a central point for many East London Mods, and became very collectable. When it was re-issued in later years however, it had lost its impetus - and then anyone could get hold of a copy, devaluing the ability of its owner to say 'I was there first'!

It was around this time that one particular group of revivalists from London adopted the title of 'Glory Boys' in favour of Mod. The reasons for this were to avoid being categorised and conditioned into becoming what many saw as a relic of the past. As far as these Glory Boys were concerned, they were a new and vibrant group who, although they acknowledged their ties with the past, were eager to move forward, and needed a name to suit. In fact, Secret Affair called their first LP Glory Boys n order to give them credability. As the ideals of all in the Mod movement were identical, this sub division was soon consumed, and blended with the rest.

A group called the Merton Parkas from Merton Park (naturally) also enjoyed a degree of chart success at this time with two of their songs - You Need Wheels, and Plastic Smile. The Merton Parkas never really became accepted as a main-stream Mod band for certain reasons of credibility that I was never fully able to fathom out. They were considered to be 'Plastic'; a term used to describe those in the new Mod movement who were only there for the ride, weren't dedicated, and didn't know what was what.

Four other bands synonymous with this new era of Modernism were The Purple Hearts, The Chords, The Mods, and Squire. Although none of these ever made much impact outside this movement, they were very popular in the confines of their own circles.

Peas of a Pod?

Something else of significant importance to youth culture was happening at this time. Not only had the Phoenix of Modernism re-emerged from the dying embers of Punk, but another cult had been given the kiss of life too. The strutting Skinhead of the late Sixties and early Seventies could now be seen everywhere. Although this figure never really disappeared and was directly responsible for the Boot Boy craze of the pre-Punk days, the Skinhead went through a very lean period during the mid Seventies. But as 1980 was embraced as the welcoming dawn of a new decade, this movement once again picked up momentum.

The build-up started around 1978, when groups like Cock Sparrer, Screwdriver, and Sham 69 (who were a major influence on the new face of Skinheadism) came to prominence, but the seeds had been sown several years earlier, during the reggae boom of 1975. Although the ancestry between Mods and Skins is almost on a par with big and baby brother, they had never before been faced by each other, and when they were, they didn't like it.

In the Sixties, they had been separated by at least two years, with Mod being the senior. Skinheadism was a natural progression from Modernism, and so when the first Skinheads came along, their predecessors had either grown up, moved on, or both. But here in the first year of the Eighties were representatives of both camps.

They were similar ages, with similar dress codes and similar tastes, and an unreconcilable void between them. They were too close for comfort and conflict was inevitable. The traditional enemy (were you to believe the press) of both these factions was the Rocker or Greaser, but in reality the main adversary for the Skinheads and the Mods was each other.

Several Mods who had adhered to the harder image of the Skinhead in preference to the stylish projection of Modernism switched their allegiances. Usually, these were the peripheral members and more often than not the 'plastics' mentioned earlier. They were shed by the Mods without any misgivings, as this was seen as the purification of the movement.

Most Skinheads at this time, unlike their originators, had no interest in scooters, and some (much to the disgust of their mentors) even went around on small capacity trials motor-cycles, although open ridicule from their counterparts soon put a stop to this.

The Skinheads who did ride around on scooters, calling themselves 'Scooter Skins', did so on standard or semi-standard machines, as the fully dressed scooters were purely the domain of the Mods. These Scooter Skins were met with caution by both the new Skinheads and Mods alike, although latterly they became an integral part of the Scootering movement.

Only in one area did Skinheads and Mods share a degree of cross-fertilisation. This was 'Two Tone' music, which had its rootes firmly placed in the Rock Steady, Ska, and Blue Beat style of reggae listened to by both groups' originators. Two Tone - like Mod and Skinhead,

Ready for Brighton: Easter 1981

had blossomed in the wake of Punk. With its recognised sound being performed by the likes of Madness, The Specials, Selector, Bad Manners, and The Beat, it was an instant success, and at that time, totally new.

Its path to prominence was pathed with people like the Clash, who, although big in Punk at that time, chose the radically different group The Specials to support them on their London's Calling tour. The Clash themselves were later to enjoy popularity among scooterists.

The name Two Tone originally came from the record label that launched the Specials and Selector, and was meant to symbolise the unification of black and white in music. Its followers named themselves after the immigrant Afro-Caribbean London Mods of the Sixties. They called themselves; 'Rude Boys, 'Rude Girls', or just plain 'Rudies', irrespective of their colour. The clothes worn by these Rudies again harped back to the Sixties, and were the same as those worn by the Mods and Skins. Items like narrow trousered dog-tooth check and tonic suits, Ben Sherman and Fred Perry shirts, thin-brimmed trilby hats (referred to as pork pie hats) and square-toed loafer shoes were favourite.

So picture if you can this precis of the situation: The Song Gangsters by the Specials and One Step Beyond by Madness had topped the charts in late '79; Sham 69's Hurry Up Harry became something of an anthen earlier in the same year, and a whole host of Modernist offerings kept popping in and out of the charts. In the space of one week, fashion turned from Disco to Dog-tooth, and from The Bee Gees to The Beat, and all that barbers were being asked for were crew cuts and crops! The whole spectrum of this social structure was epitomised perfectly by the Leyton Buzzards and their vaguely satirical song Saturday Night Beneath The Plastic Palm Trees. So the stage was set. Act one scene one was over, but what was in store for scene two?

Two's a Crowd, Three's Terrible

There was a definite need for consolidation. Two's company and three's a crowd. Purely because of the tribal nature of the beast, this eternal triangle of cultural incest could not be tolerated for long. As Modernism and Skinheadism were the two most clearly definable camps of the three, it was the members of the middle ground, the Rudies and the followers of Two Tone who were going to have to give. There was no conscious effort to dissipate these followers, as natural selection appeared to rear its head, helping those concerned to subconsciously decide on which side of the fence they felt their allegiances lay.

Those who had adopted an affiliation for the Sixties and scooters joined the march of the Mods, while those with a preference for soccer and Ska became staunch Skinheads. Some gave up this style of sub-culture completely, and others floated carefully between the two. The music too, was forced to take sides, and soon settled for Skinheadism. It wasn't to enjoy unified recognition again until the amalgamated group labelled Scooter Boys was to find its feet in the Spring of '82.

Slowly, the differences in appearance between Mods and the Skinheads widened. Whereas previously most Skins and Mods had worn their hair grade four length (about half an inch long), the Skins now preferred grade one crops (practically shaven). The Mods on the other hand allowed their hair to lengthen slightly and sported side-parted college boy cuts. Some even back-combed their hair and cultivated a central 'French line' parting, as styled by Paul Weller who along with his band The Jam were going from strength to strength, and unwittingly setting standards of style and dress. Clothing, too, started to differ, as Mods turned more casual, and the Skins reverted to a more unified boots and braces image. The only garment which continually enjoyed popularity across the board was the olive-green American MA1 flying jacket, which was to stay in vogue and become the recognised symbol of the scooterist.

The 'In' Crowd

By the end of 1980, the scooter-riding Mod revivalist was well established, and like his ancestors, had a particularly healthy fashion scene. New styles would (as they had in the Sixties) come and go week by week, and sometimes day by day. This aspect of Modernism was slightly lost in later years, as uniformity crept in - stan-dardising styles, and making obsolete the innovative 'Face'.

Brighton, Easter 1981

Brighton, Easter 1981

I can still vividly recall visiting Barrons, a puritan Sixties night club in Leigh-on-Sea, near Southend in Essex. You were expected to turn up on your suitably trimmed scooter (in my case a 1962 Vespa Sportique 150cc) at least half an hour before the doors opened and strut around the car park with your parka removed (so long as it wasn't raining) like a model on a cat walk. You would allow yourself and your scooter to be scrutinised, while tentatively studying others. This wasn't done clinically, as you would talk, laugh and chat amongst your fellow Mods, but all the time you'd be clocking what's what! Parallel pastel hipsters, suede brogues and tight turtle neck sweaters could be in one week - then cords, bowling shoes and cycling shirts the next.

The only thing you could really be sure of were suede and leather box jackets, as these cost so much they were always acceptable. You didn't have time to get bored. The constant rejuvenation of image left you in a swirl. It was exciting, exhilarating and extremely expensive, but I and many others loved it. If you couldn't keep up, you had to keep out. Unfortunately, it was this last train of thought that was to bring about this wave's downfall. Elitism became rife, alienating many whose hearts were in the right place. It was the prolonged paisley-peacock period of mid '81 before most people managed to catch up, but by then it was too late. There was a need for something new!

By the Christmas 1981 there appeared to be three separate camps emerging from the mainstream of Mod. These became more apparent in the first months of 1982. Those motivated wholly by the ever changing image had moved on via natural transgression to the next fashionable phase after paisley: Psychedelia. Closely resembling the trendy dandies from whom the Hippie boom had taken off at the end of the Sixties, this faction soon went their own separate way, and in time fizzled out. A cultural back-lash caused many to return to the more traditional image of Modernism through the re-introduction of suits, while the third main group seemed to settle for a more contemporary and casual style of dress as they gravitated closer to the scooter. With their walking-out wardrobe centred virtually entirely around jeans, denim jackets, olive green American MA1 bomber jackets (which soon gained the nick-name of Scooter Jackets), and an assortment of foot wear such as Base-Ball, Boxing, Monkey, and later Doctor Martin boots, they could still be seen as part of the Mod movement, although starting to follow a different path.

Keep On Keeping On

The Lean Years

During the Seventies, the popularity of the scooter slipped into a definite decline. They were no longer the machines of the moment, as the Japanese were more than adequately catering for the commuter market. The last Italian-made Lambrettas - the GP range, had come and gone at the turn of the decade, and Vespa's UK sales dropped considerably.

The scooter had gone from being 'hip' in the Sixties, to being frankly ridiculous in the Seventies. This was the period of the 'Easy Riders' style of Biker, with large capacity 'chopper' motor-cycles being the fashionable two-wheeled machines of the day - although very few people actually owned one. But as with all things which once touched the hearts of a nation, the scooter wasn't allowed to disappear completely. It had found its devotees, who although low in numbers, ensured the scooter's preservation.

These enthusiasts jelled themselves into scooter clubs, and were supported by the long-established owners' organisations of both Lambrettas and Vespas. They arranged various activities such as the sporting trials which had been going since the Fifties, small scale sea-side runs, and race meetings - all activities which still happen today.

In some areas however - predominantly in the North, the scooter still enjoyed a degree of cult status. This was not because its disciples were behind the times, but because the sounds they adhered to allowed certain aspects of Modernism to continue.

The music they listened to was closely based on Sixties styled Soul, but it had been developed irrespective of national pop trends throughout the Seventies into something new. It was peculiar to the North, and could be heard in all of its major trendy night clubs. Although its performers were largely American, its categorising title was derived from its first region of recognition; it was known as 'Northern Soul', and The Wigan Casino became its Mecca.

This is Soul.

Northern Soul music was not only for the ears of the Seventies styled scooterist. Its followers came from a much wider catchment of cults and soon, it too became a movement in its own right. Rarity and originality became the Northern Soul followers' order of the day. Not in dress - as with the Sixties soul fans - but in the ownership of exclusive records.

In order for Northern Soul's DJs and record collectors to keep their credence, they had to be constantly unearthing new sounds. These were either freshly discovered Sixties soul songs, or newly released tracks from the USA. Also, in time, Britain came up with its own Northern Soul performers.

One such singer went by the name of Lenny Gamble, and released a passable version of Doris Troy's song; I'll Do Anything. This particular recording - which later appeared on a Casino Classics compilation album - became quite popular in Northern Soul circles. However, had the true identity of its singer been known, I doubt anyone would've listened to it at all. For Lenny Gamble and the then Radio One DJ Tony Blackburn, were one and the same!

Britain's Billy Ocean had a hit on both the Northern and national scene in '76 with his song Love Really Hurts Without You, and a cover of the Rolling Stones song Under My Thumb by Wayne Gibson enjoyed an airing in '74. Another home-grown group - Wigan's Chosen Few, entered the national charts in the early Seventies with an instrumental called Footsie. When performed on Top Of The Pops it was accompanied by a dance troupe fresh from The Casino who were dressed to thrill.

These dancers were both athletic and acrobatic. They performed back-flips, spins, high kicks, and intricately stepped foot work, all linked together in a breath-taking display. This dancing became the physical pursuit of the Northern Soul follower, although not all were as agile as the Chosen Few.

The clothes they wore were Oxford bag trousers which flared out from the hips, a selection of tight fitting

V-necked jumpers, and an assortment of large-collared casual shirts. Not only were these garments the fashion of the day, but, in time, they became the uniform of the Northern Souly - along with printed vest tops, and flat slip-on shoes.

This indigenous dance music of the North thrived on obscurity. When a song became too popular or common, it was dropped like a hot brick. Because of this, rare and new discs would have their centres covered by pasted-on paper circles. This was done to avoid fellow collectors or DJs discovering the identity of the singer, the record label it appeared on, and sometimes even the name of the song itself. In this way, the origin of a good and catchy tune could be kept secret longer, thus lengthening its dance floor life.

Something Old, Something New

In late '78, the name Mod had two distinctive - and equally valid interpretations. In the South, the mainstay of Modernists were from the revivalist school, while in the North they were more influenced by the on-going face of scootering. In short, the revivalists created the Southern scene, while they just swelled the ranks of those in the North.

By the early Eighties, both camps of Modernism - seen by most outsiders as being one and the same, were making the papers. With the return of massed Mod migrations to coastal resorts over Bank Holiday week-ends, the press resurrected the tales of teenage terror which had sold newspapers in the Sixties.

They started reporting on fictitious clashes between rival gangs of Mods and Rockers. By doing this, they fanned the flames of a dormant feudal fire. Fortunately, all they managed to do was make the smouldering embers glow and flicker. Although several such skirmishes did occur, the majority of the aggression seldom manifested itself as anything more than bouts of cat calling.

The Mods down South congregated in towns such as Clacton, Margate, Brighton, and Southend for their scooter runs, while those up North preferred places like Skegness and Scarborough. Because of regional differences, these two sections of Modernism hardly ever

The Burnley and Pendle Scooter Club, Late '70s

The York Scooter Day, Early '80s

met. When they did, their differences became clearly apparent.

Two Faced Mods.

It was the August Bank Holiday of 1979 when I first became aware of the two separate schools involved within Modernism. Until that time I had thought nothing of it, thinking these strange scooterists from the north-lands to be nothing more than out of touch and plastic. It took a further three years before I finally saw the error of my ways.

Over the weekend in question, the Lambretta Club of Great Britain had arranged for a members-only rally to be held on Leigh Island just outside Southend in Essex. However, due to the power of the scooter riders' grapevine, far more than those expected were destined to attend.

Scootering Mods from all over the UK converged on an unsuspecting Southend on the Saturday and Sunday immediately preceeding the Bank Holiday Monday. The revivalists - all suitably dressed - couldn't fathom out the Northern lads, who were wearing giant flares and listening to music more reminiscent of Seventies' disco than The Yardbirds or The Rolling Stones.

To each other, they appeared to be as different as chalk and cheese. Something would have to happen. There was no way they could share the same name. Only the Parka and the similarly trimmed scooters unified them. But this, too, would in time change.

Time For Action

The majority of Mod scooter rallies in 1980 were regional, and operated on a 'pirate'-run basis. They were arranged by word of mouth, and only attracted numbers in the high hundreds. The rallies of '81, too, were predominantly organised by word of mouth, but for the first time they became more national, and weren't just restricted to the Bank Holiday weekends. These innovations were poached - if not actually introduced - by the Lambretta Club of Great Britain who promoted many of the early scooter runs.

Margate, Whitsun 1981

Because of these new practices, Mods from all over met at the various resorts around the country where nationally organised rallies were being held. This enabled the slow integration between North and South to begin, although the odd incident of late-night beer talk hindered the unification process slightly. However, all that could ever really be hoped for was an acceptance of one another.

The neatly groomed revivalists found it very difficult to adhere to the Northern scooterists, who by now were wearing Doctor Martin boots, ex-army drill trousers, and faded denim jackets emblazoned with brightly-coloured scooter rally patches. It was thought they'd gone too far.

Their scooters, too, started to differ in their adornment. Whereas the revivalists still added quantities of chromed accessories to personalise their machines, those following the continuation of scootering from the Seventies started to favour a different approach.

Their ideas on customising centred on the bodywork, and incorporated intricate air-brushed murals, and occasionally cut-away panels. The extras they preferred were the 'bubble' style of fly-screen, and the reversible flip-flop back rest. All these trends stood the test of time, and were represented at rallies throughout the Eighties.

The main places these two factions met during '81 were Great Yarmouth - which hosted annual national rallies throughout the Eighties, Bournemouth - for possibly the wettest rally ever, and old the faithful - Brighton, where three separate scooter rallies took place throughout the year. These were two regional Bank Holiday Mod runs - one at Easter, and one in August, and a national rally in June.

The first signs of capitulation from the revivalists came when certain groups started to form scooter clubs in preference to gangs. Although such clubs were nothing new, they were an integral part of the Seventies scooter scene, and showed a deeper commitment towards the scooter as their main cult focal point.

This was exactly the same ethos which influenced the Northern scooterists' mode of dress. With the scooter taking the lead roll, their clothing requirements changed considerably, allowing items more practical for riding in to enter the frame. The rally patches they wore became their campaign medals, and were a visual display of their stalwart dedication and experience.

Margate 1981

It was this facet of scootering's new face which attracted many of those becoming bored with mainstream Mod. It allowed them to pursue their love of the scooter without having to participate in the rat race of elitist fashion.

By 1982, the gap between the two interpretations of Modernism had widened further. It was no longer represented by a North and South divide, but by the two conflicting images of those involved. They started congregating accordingly. About 1,000 revivalists made their way down to Hastings in Sussex for a Mod run over the Easter Bank Holiday weekend, while 3,000 others clad in an assortment of olive drab army surplus rode to Scarborough in Yorkshire for a scooter rally organised by the Lambretta Club of Great Britain.

It was while in Scarborough that the final and conclusive split between the two scootering factions became apparent. Since the Fifties, there had been a name banded about by members of the general public to describe the youths of their areas who whizzed around on scooters. This name never disappeared. It was always there floating around the fringes of the scootering fraternity.

In order to disassociate themselves from the revivalists who tended to be a few years younger than them, this was the title these new national scooter riders adopted. Many had been using it for years, but Scarborough '82 saw scooterists gathering en mass under this banner for the first time. They called themselves 'Scooter Boys'!

Let The Good Times Roll

Keep On Runnin'

1982 saw another major mile-stone being laid towards a united and national scootering movement. Martin Dixon, a resident of Scarborough and editor of Scootermania - a popular A5 fanzine of the early eighties, joined forces with several individuals from the Lambretta Club and set about arranging the year's rallies via democratic voting.

Between them, they compiled a list of British scooter clubs. At the beginning of the year, they invited a representative from each of these to attend a Pow-Wow at which the venues and dates for the year's scooter runs would be decided. As those who turned up were more often than not the main members of their clubs, this meeting was called simply The Number Ones, and was held annually there after.

Although in the early days the various club's number twos, threes and occasionally fours tended to turn up for these meetings - causing more than just a little confusion, the details were always settled before the evening's festivities commenced. These consisted of scooterist-styled discos and parties for all concerned and marked the start of the new scootering year.

The fine tuning for the forthcoming rallies was then left to those voted in by the Number Ones (Twos and Threes). Collectively, this governing body became known as the National Runs Committee - the NRC.

The '82 rally season started - as stated - in Scarborough, and came to a close with Whitley Bay in October. But between these, the active members of this newly-defined national scooterist movement - the Scooter Boys - visited Loch Lomond, Great Yarmouth, Morecambe Bay, Brighton, Colwyn Bay, the Isle of Wight, and Skegness.

With perhaps the exception of Loch Lomond, which was fraught with problems and poorly attended, all these rallies went down well. For many - myself included - they offered continual adventure, a new-found direction, and a much maligned sense of belonging. The mobile scooterists of Britain could no longer be content with the confines of their own home towns and counties.

Scooter Boys - and girls - wanted to travel, see other parts of the country, meet its people, party with others sharing their ideals, and live life to the full. Through scooter runs, they could do this. Their movement's growth in popularity was guaranteed.

Rallies also offered these youths a degree of temporary escapism from the hum-drum toil of daily life. With nothing more than a sleeping bag and a tent tied to their scooters, they could dissapear for a couple of days, and return spiritually refreshed.

The weeks between rallies were filled by meetings with fellow local scooterists to talk scooters, to drink, dance, and generally make merry - while oozing enthusiasm for their chosen life-style. But all the time they would be counting down the days until the next national run.

As the pre-destined weekend for a rally drew ever closer, the excitement in the Scooter Boys' veins would heighten - reaching a crescendo on the day of departure. These feelings of exhilaration never floundered, and continued to provide the main driving force and motivation for each road-going and rallying Scooterist throughout their individual period of involvement.

The Good the Bad and the Practical

The Mod movement - although marginally lower in numbers than the Scooter Boy scene - embraced 1984 by holding its own version of the Number Ones meeting. Their members, too, came from a national catchment, and demanded Mod rallies accordingly. These were organised initially by the Phoenix Society, and latterly by the Classic Club International. Invariably they visited the same venues as the Scooter Boys, but never over the same weekends.

The reasons for needing two separate sets of scootering-orientated national rallies had materialised the previous year. Numbers on the pirate rally scene - the forum for the Mods, had dwindled considerably, and only tended to cater for those in the Home Counties.

Because of this many Mods had started attending the national scooter rallies. This cramped their style considerably, as it meant rubbing shoulders with the new breed of Scooter Boy - who they saw as being scruffy and unkempt.

Constantly wanting to disassociate themselves from the Mod image, and striving for pastures new, the Scooter Boys, too, took a dim view of the Mods' presence, and a degree of animosity developed. Segregation became essential for their co-existence.

The Mod movement tapered off slightly as the Eighties rolled on, but it never disappeared. Instead it consolidated - adding Latin and raw Blues music to its repertoire of acceptable sounds.

With the Scooter Boy scene being well established by 1983/4, green recruits opting to enter the world of scootering were no longer limited to the fashions of Modernism. A passion for scooters was sufficient.

Whereas in 1979 a potential teenage scooter enthusiast would buy a scoot, a Sixties-styled suit, and plenty of mirrors and lights, they would now be more likely to resemble an extra from M*A*S*H as they saddled their standard steeds. The Scooter Boys' image had a far greater and wider-ranging appeal.

Clothing requirements gravitated more and more towards practicality for the Scooter Boy, as the importance of riding to rallies became all-important. Full-faced crash helmets and leather motor-cycle jackets no longer brought open ridicule - as they had with the Mods, while sturdy and effective water-proofs replaced the highly inadequate Parka.

The Scooter Boys' clothes were not always worn in a shapeless manner (except the water-proofs!), and helped create their acceptable style. As with all fashions born out of practicality, it looked good and lasted. Occasionally this image would be flaunted, advertising the Scooter Boys divorce from Mod - although for most members of the general public the subtlety of this action was wasted. As far as they were conserned, all and sundry driving scooters were delinquent Mods. Your average Joe Soap was beyond re-education.

The lack of fashionable restrictions among members of the scootering movement allowed followers of many other youth cults to become involved, bringing with them yet further innovations. If favoured, these were readily accepted, although the Scooter Boys' nucleus of Northern Soul and scooters remained unchanged.

Skinheads riding scooters finally gained acceptance and re-introduced the trends of closely cropped hair and Two-Tone music. The Punks brought with them 'Alternative' music from bands like The Clash, The Sex Pistols, and The Buzzcocks - while the Rockabillies and Psychobillies offered exaggerated quiffs, flat tops, Fifties 'Fun Rock' and the peculiar music of King Kurt and the Meteors.

The latter of these, however, with its accompanying 'Slam Dancing', lost its main stream appeal towards the end of '87. At first, Psychobilly was seen as entertainingly diverse and fun. But after a mere three years of across-the-board acceptability, many started to consider it as passe and corny. Only its most avid of scootering supporters continued to listen to it, although this brought them much criticism - albeit behind their backs.

All Day and all of the Night

Scooter rallies had more than one high-light. The first of these came from the thrill of riding to a rally amid a pack of scooterists from your local area. Invariably you would know one another at the outset of your voyage, but after several arduous hours on the road together, you'd be like brothers. The camaraderie played no small part in creating the perfect atmosphere before you even reached your desired destinations.

The longer the journey, the more you'd get to know one another. In this way, friendships were formed which would last indefinitely. The best - and most genuine friends I've ever made, were met through such journeys, as after sharing numerous wrong turnings and breakdowns together, your true colours couldn't help but shine through.

Punctuated by regular pub and grub stops, such trips were almost enough in themselves, but the best was yet to come. As you drew near the town staging the rally in question, you'd start noticing - with increasing frequency - concentrations of others doing the same.

Your various routes would merge into one, ending in a continous stream of scooters pouring through a town's boundaries.

Occasionally police road blocks pulled over those hoping to attend a particular rally, just before the point of no return, and checked their documents for any irregularities. But on the whole the scooterist was allowed to pass in peace,

If the scooterists in attendance were lucky enough to be entering a town with an accommodating council, hand-hewn signs could be found directing them to the official scooter rally campsite. In this way, the pillars of seaside society could be assured their peace, knowing wayward Scooter Boys wouldn't desecrate their particular streets in the early hours of the morning looking for somewhere to sleep.

Those who didn't follow these signs tended to be the more affluent members of the scooter riding fraternity who went in search of Bed And Breakfast accommodation instead. Such creature comforts were usually cheap enough for the odd weekend of self indulgence, and increased in popularity as the winter months approached.

Friday was always arrival day. Depending on the length of their journey, and number of obstacles encountered, the majority of rally patrons would arrive between tea-time on day one, and breakfast on the following morning. Although exhausted from their trips, adrenalin blocked out the more rational instinct of resting.

Because of this, once their weekend habitations had been sorted, and suitable opportunities made themselves available, the Scooter Boy would go in search of the good times. Sleep wasn't important. There would be plenty of time in the following week to catch up on that, but for now they wanted to party. And that's exactly what they did.

With the exception of an in-land rally to Newark in Nottinghamshire during June '84, all these national scooter runs took place near coastal towns. The camp-sites provided for these rallies, ranged from appalling in Skegness and Redcar, to fantastic at Exmouth. Their entry fees, too, differed quite considerably. They went from free, to fair, to 'How Much!' - depending on who-ever was behind its organisation.

Often, the councils of the various venues hosting a rally would police the designated camping areas themselves. At other times the National Runs Committee were asked to do so, and occasionally - as on the Isle of Wight, outside promoters would be given the franchise.

The promenade and assorted amusement arcades along the sea fronts of these towns, would be alive with activity over rally weekends. Scooters would be constantly zipping around, dodging jay-walking pedestrians, while other scooterists would be congregating around the various pubs and clubs, waiting for the onslaught of the lunch-time session.

The numbers of Scooter Boys attending these rallies throughout the Eighties was staggering. At the bottom of the scale were the Scottish runs which attracted around 2,000 or so after 1982; and reaching somewhere in the region of 12,000 at the largest rally ever - on the Isle of Wight at August Bank Holiday, 1984. An average of 5,000 attended the majority of the runs, but those coinciding with Bank Holidays, always attracted more.

It was because of the sheer volume of people involved with the scooter rally scene, that several promoters started offering entertainment on the runs. The best known of these was Chris Burton who with his company, Torch Promotions, arranged - initially with the approval of the NRC - the bulk of 'On The Run' musical activities.

These took the form of lunch-time and evening discos, which would be held in an assortment of night clubs and or civic halls leased to the promoters over the weekends in question. Before the all-day licensing law changes of '88, the daytime dos usually ran from twelve 'til three, but the evening entertainments lasted much longer.

An integral part of the Seventies Northern Soul scene had been the longevity of its discos. These ran right through the night, ending at breakfast time the next day, and were known as 'Allniters'. With their first choice in music actually being Northern Soul, it was only natural for such functions to be picked up on by the Scooter Boys. Allniters became firmly instilled as an official rally pursuit. Promoters provided them accordingly when ever possible.

In order to maintain the Allniters' popularity, and ensure good attendance (and profits) on the runs, the people behind them didn't rely on DJs alone. They

Edwin Starr

Desmond Dekker

Buster Bloodvessel of Bad Manners

started putting on star performer attractions from the world of scootering. These consisted of live performances from people such as Desmond Dekker, Edwin Starr, King Kurt (when in vogue), Eddie Holman, and Bad Manners, just to name a few.

This innovation meant that the rally-goer could be ensured an evening of first class entertainment. But because of such concerts, by the mid-Eighties many non-scootering types had started attending the runs, purely for the musical entertainment. This came to a head in 1986 and brought about a dramatic change in the structuring of national scooter rallies, but more about that later.

With an assortment of scootering-orientated traders setting up stalls on the various scooter rally campsites - selling everything from spares to clothing, and a scooter custom show usually taking place on the last full day, the hours between discos were packed with things to do. However, if the weather was good, lounging around in the sun took precedence - allowing for rest and recuperation, ready for the next taxing bout of revelry.

This pattern of events would continue until the last day of the rally which - depending on whether it had been a Bank Holiday or weekend run - would be either the Sunday or Monday. There would then be a massed exodus of homeward bound Scooter Boys and Girls, which was normally complete by midday.

The afflicted towns could then return to normal, and their publicans and caterers count their money. Despite the outrage of some inconvenienced inhabitants, the hosting of a rally could often be the the saviour of many small businesses. With the increasing annual migration of holiday-making sun-seekers to the continent, many indigenous British coastal resorts started to suffer. An influx of scooterists could re-float their flagging economy.

A landlord with whom I became particularly friendly at Great Yarmouth, once showed me his weekend takings after a rally. Never before, or since, have I seen so much hard cash in one lump sum. In his safe he had no less than £23,000! And he was not alone. With an average of 5,000 scooterists attending most national rallies - and each spending in the region of £50, even those without a head for figures could see that entertaining Scooter Boys was most definitely a viable proposition.

Rolling Back The Years

1988 and '89 only saw eight national rallies each, but the years from '82 through held no less than nine. These took place at a variety of venues, some on a regular basis, and some only the once. The break-down of these is as follows:

1982
Scarborough -- Easter Bank Holiday
Loch Lomond -- May Bank Holiday
Great Yarmouth -- Whitsun Bank Holiday
Morecambe Bay -- Late June
Brighton -- Mid July
Colwyn Bay -- Early August
Isle of Wight -- August Bank Holiday
Skegness -- Mid September
Whitley Bay -- Early October

1983
Morecambe Bay -- Easter Bank Holiday
Weymouth -- May Bank Holiday
Great Yarmouth -- Whitsun Bank Holiday
Dunbar -- Mid June
Weston Super Mare -- Early July
Scarborough -- Early August
Isle of Wight -- August Bank Holiday
Southport -- Mid September
Skegness -- Early October

1984
Morecambe Bay -- Easter Bank Holiday
Torquay -- May Bank Holiday
Great Yarmouth -- Whitsun Bank Holiday
Newark -- Late June
Dunbar -- Mid July
Colwyn Bay -- Early August
Isle of Wight -- August Bank Holiday
Weston Super Mare -- Mid September
Skegness -- Early October

1985

Morecambe Bay -- Easter Bank Holiday
Clacton -- May Bank Holiday
Great Yarmouth -- Whitsun Bank Holiday
Dunbar -- Late June
Exmouth -- Early July
Colwyn Bay -- Early August
Isle of Wight -- August Bank Holiday
Weston Super Mare -- Mid September
Redcar -- Early October

1986

Great Yarmouth -- Easter Bank Holiday
Morecambe Bay -- May Bank Holiday
Margate -- Whitsun Bank Holiday
Exmouth -- Mid June
Porthcawl -- Early July
Girvan -- Late July
Isle of Wight -- August Bank Holiday
Rhyl -- Mid September
Scarborough -- Mid October

1987

Morecambe Bay -- Easter Bank Holiday
Great Yarmouth -- May Bank Holiday
Isle of Wight -- Whitsun Bank Holiday
Girvan -- Mid June
Rhyl -- Early July
Margate -- Late July, early August
Scarborough -- August Bank Holiday
Weston Super Mare -- Late September
Newquay -- Mid October

1988

Isle of Wight -- Easter Bank Holiday
Great Yarmouth -- May Bank Holiday
Scarborough -- Whitsun Bank Holiday
Exmouth -- Mid June
Margate -- Late July
Morecambe Bay -- August Bank Holiday
Aberystwyth -- Mid September
Weston Super Mare -- Mid October

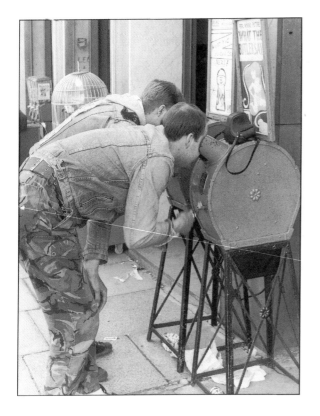

1989
Isle of Wight -- Easter Bank Holiday
Great Yarmouth -- May Bank Holiday
Fort William -- Whitsun Bank Holiday
Whitley Bay -- Mid June
Exmouth -- Early July
Aberystwyth -- Late July
Morecambe Bay -- August Bank Holiday
Margate -- Late September

Although these were the all-important rallies for the Scooter Boy, they weren't the only ones which attracted large numbers. Each year, three weeks or so after the last national rally, members of the North West Alliance - instigated by the Stockport Crusaders scooter club, arranged and held an 'End of Year' run.

The first of these I attended was held at Blackpool back in '82. Other locations used through the Eighties included Rhyl, Morecambe Bay, Colwyn Bay, and Llandudno. Another major promoter of large scale scooter runs in the mid Eighties was Vespa UK. On non-conflicting national rally weekends, they held two of the biggest scootering events of their respective years. These were the Donnington International Scooter Classic - June 8th/9th 1986 (DISC '86) held at Donnington Park, and the Doncaster International Scooter Classic - August 1st/2nd 1987 (DISC '87) held at the Doncaster Race Course. The high point of DISC '86 was an open-air late-night performance by Bad Manners - among other bands in a star-studded line-up. At DISC '87, it was a similar gig headed up by Desmond Dekker.

The Eighties also saw the growth in popularity of continental Vespa runs. These took place in Spain, Germany, Austria, Belgium, Switzerland, and France. The numbers of British Scooter Boys attending these rallies grew each and every year. An International Lambretta rally, too, was held in 1989 at Strasbourg, but proved to be a bit of a flop.

Patching Up The Past

Tales of their various trials and tribulations, in the form of embroidered anecdotes about scooter rallies, made up the majority of the Scooter Boys' and Girls' late night club conversations when meeting a new

group of fellow scooterists for the first time. Although the main motivation behind such stories was provisionally to entertain, they had another purpose which was far more important.

They - in a light-hearted way, proved the orator's commitment to the scootering way of life, and emphasised their credibility by spelling out - quite literally, which and exactly how many scooter runs they had attended. Another way in which many Scooter Boys proved their pedigree was with tattoos. These took the form of scooter club logos - as on their respective members patches, or as was more often the case, Lambretta and Vespa crests.

Small silver and gold scooter charms were also worn - either on a chain around the neck, or dangling from the obligatorily pierced left ear. But by far the most popular, and integral method of displaying dedication, was derived from the cloth patch - as worn by this movement's mentors.

As early as 1980 individuals involved with the Scooter Boy scene started selling screen-printed patches as mementoes of rally weekends. Along with copies of scooter club patches, which were sold in order to raise funds, these were freely available by mid '82.

Procuring such patches became almost as important to the rally- goer, as the run itself. Once sewn to their MA1 or Levi jackets, they provided visual proof of clubs they had met, and runs attended. However, as many of the patch retailers were only doing so to make a few bob, any of these they had left over at one meeting would be offered for sale at the next. This practice was fine for the club patches, but was disapproved of when it came to those for the rallies.

With such items being on offer at an assortment of gatherings, anyone could obtain them at any time. This devalued their ability to prove categorically that the wearer had actually been to the run in question. Because of this, one scooterist started producing the definitive rally patch in 1983. These were only available at the relevant times, cost a mere fifty pence, and were numbered and dated accordingly.

Named after their manufacturer - Paddy Smith - they soon became the only rally patch to own, and were available throughout the Eighties. Stalwart Scooter Boys collected their 'Paddy Smith's' with fervour, and arranged them in rows on their jackets. These four

A selection of Paddy Smith patches

inch-square pieces of cloth became the ultimate proof of where a scooterist had been and when. But not all chose to follow this trend. The older and more established Scooter Boys, of whom there were many, often left their jackets plain. They did this for three main reasons: Firstly, If they had already filled a jacket with patches, but had subsequently grown out of it, they didn't want another. Secondly, many disliked the inescapable symmetry created by rows of Paddy Smith's - preferring patches of varying sizes as seen in the early days. And thirdly, with a good few active scootering years under their collective belts, they couldn't care who thought where they'd been, and when!

Scooter Boys

Scooter Boys   81

Scooter Boys

Scooter Boys

Scooter Boys

Scooter Boys

　　　　　　　　　　　Scooter Boys

Scooter Boys

Scooter Boys

Scooter Boys

Scooter Boys

Scooter Boys

Scooter Boys

Scooter Boys

Scooter Boys

Scooter Boys

Scooter Boys 105

Something Better Change

Island in the Sun

Successful scooter rallies were held on the Isle of Wight over August Bank Holiday weekends from 1981 to '85. The first of these - attracting around 800, was, relatively speaking, very small indeed. But by 1982 - the first year of the amalgamated Scooter Boy movement - things had changed considerably.

In this year the Smallbrook stadium near Ryde was the designated camping area. With about 2,500 Scooter Boys and Mods camping around its cinder running-track over a sun-soaked Bank Holiday weekend, this run was first class; refreshing, and at that time all new. On this occasion, the evening's entertainment took place in the Carousel club a couple of miles away. The DJ - Tony Class, whose signature tune was Be Young, be Foolish, and be Happy by the Tamms, whipped everyone up in to an emotional frenzy.

1983 was a carbon copy of '82, except that the numbers had doubled, and those calling themselves Mods halved. By 1984, the promoters behind the Isle of Wight run had moved the venue to a rented farm of some considerable acreage in anticipation of a larger number of patrons. This proved to be a good move as an estimated 12,000 turned up, many of whom arrived on the island during the week before for a holiday - the rally being the climax.

Being early arrivals for this rally, my club members and I, sat around watching the thousands of scooters spewing through the gates well into the night. The continual stream of glowing headlamps didn't let up until sunrise Saturday morning. With a sizeable beer tent, and an assortment of caterers on site, the atmosphere was indescribable. For us, this was it. Nothing could surpass this experience. We felt completely

Homeward bound after an Isle-of-Wight rally

elated. An open air concert By Edwin Starr - shared with a writhing mass of scooterists, just added the finishing touch to what had been the perfect rally weekend.

Another annual pleasure associated with the Isle of Wight came when homeward bound. As the ferries returning Scooter Boys (as most were by then) to the mainland came within striking distance of Portsmouth or Southampton, each of the two hundred or so scooters on board, would fire up ... and by the time the ferry actually docked everyone's eyes would be smarting from the concentration of two-stroke fumes. But as the landing ramp went down, the cloud of blue smoke would bellow out in front of the awaiting car passengers, accompanied by the revving of engines and drone of horns. Then, out of this noisy cloud we would ride in one large mass, like an invading army. The incredulous stares from the on-lookers of this spectacle were priceless. What a feeling: Absolutely Fantastic!

'85 saw another venue of a similar size, but this soon turned into a mud bath after hours of torrential rain on the Friday. This rally - although still enjoyable, carried for the first time the signs of things to come. With an even larger line-up of live star performers - including several Skin Head 'Oi' bands not usually connected with scootering, it soon became apparent that many present were not scooterists, and were there purely for the music.

As Scooter Skins had been absorbed by the Scooter Boy - bringing with them the fashion of closely cropped hair, many non-scootering Skin Heads were able to infiltrate the scene virtually without detection. As the vast majority of scooterists were patriotic, and wore items incorporating the Union Jack, the fanatical fascist politics of these non-scooter riding Skins, too, at first went unnoticed.

By the time their presence was felt, it was too late. Persuading them to leave was bound to cause an ugly scene. At the Great Yarmouth rally in '86, a group of racialist Skin Heads attacked Desmond Dekker during an Allniter in Tiffany's. They caused a disturbance at Margate, and were bound to turn up again.

The Isle-of-Wight 1987

The Isle of Wight 1986

The last national August Bank Holiday scooter rally to the Isle of Wight, took place on an assortment of adjoining fields near Newport in 1986. The number of people on this site was in the region of 10,000, while another small group of scooterists headed by the National Runs committee, held an alternative run near Ryde. They did this for a number of political reasons, which in the event proved to be a good move. Because of certain undertones, the NRC wanted to totally disassociate themselves from the large rally's promoter. But most Scooter Boys who - like me, had put the annual Isle of Wight rally on a pedestal, ignored the NRCs request to boycott the main site, and camped on it anyway.

The Friday night saw many thousands of tents being hurriedly erected, while countless columns of scooters queued to gain entry. Again all the signs were there to indicate that this would be an excellent rally, but by Sunday that would all change. Already annoyed by the increased entry fee which was considered too high, further discontent came from the rising prices of the on-site caterers. But at this stage it wasn't too big a problem. Friday and Saturday were thoroughly enjoyable, with plenty of scooterists' camaraderie, and another excellent performance by Edwin Starr, amidst occasional downpours. Sunday, too, for the main part went well, but in the evening, the congenial atmosphere dissolved.

The bands booked to play on the Sunday night were The Business, Condemned '84, and Vicious Rumours. All these were Oi bands with dubious political ideals, and were not welcome by the Scooter Boys. Throughout the afternoon a steady stream of pedestrian non-scootering Skinheads had arrived - attracted purely by the prospect of a live performance by these groups. Unlike the previous evening, which had seen thousands of dancing, partying scooterists congregated in front of the massive open-air stage, this selection of gigs were played to a couple of hundred only - those who had turned up specially.

For the main part, most of the 10,000 Scooter Boys and Girls present formed themselves into sizeable groups, and either sat around an assortment of campfires, or stood within sight of the stage while just drinking and talking. They weren't enjoying the music being played, and tried their best to shut it out. When the sounds stopped around midnight, things started to happen: Fed up with the price of the on-site booze, which had more than doubled inside twenty four hours, a group of people raided the beer tent. This grew in magnitude as - upon hearing about it - hundreds and hundreds of scooterists joined them. The tent's staff fled, leaving everything, resulting in yet more looting. With the beer gone, attention switched to the caterers who too had been inflating their prices by the hour. But then far more sinister implications arose.

Some-one set fire to the large and now empty drinks marquee. Within seconds it was engulfed with flames, and the gas canisters inside started exploding. A large group gathered to watch, as the Fire Brigade came to take control. But a gang of Skinheads appeared, and started stoning the firemen, who were forced to make a hasty retreat. A van load of riot police were treated similarly and, too, withdrew. The safety services then refused to enter the fields in question which were illuminated by an orange glow from the still-flaming fire. For the following five hours, anarchy reined supreme.

The rioting mob then started indiscriminately turning over food vans and looting scooter trader's stalls. Vicious fighting broke out between rival groups without the law to intervene, and many scooterists fled the field. As the sun rose at six, the police - suitably reinforced - moved in. But the main perpetrators of the previous evenings disturbances had long since gone. All that was left were a couple of thousand bewildered scooterists, who - now sober - were preparing for the off. Realising that these were not the instigators of the problems, the police let these pass in peace, but many were searched at the terminals before boarding the ferries.

The last two rallies of '86 - to Rhyl and Scarborough, were relatively trouble free and were organised by the NRC. The Number Ones meeting that followed introduced measures ensuring such an incident could never happen again.

Drastic Measures for Drastic Needs

Since the creation of the national rally scene, the dates and venues of where to go and when had been freely available, allowing for promoters and non-scooterists to plan their attendance well in advance. This information was initially available through a selection of small-scale scooter-orientated fanzines, and, after its launch in May '85, could be found in the only nationally distributed scooterists' magazine of that time - Scootering. This was all to change.

The National Runs Committee (which changed its name to The National Scooter Riders Association in 1989) decided after a series of democratic votes involving members of the Number Ones, that starting with the 1987 season, all such information should be kept secret. No outside promoters should be allowed to become involved, and no more star attractions would be invited to play on the runs. In this way they felt that scootering could get back to its roots.

The relevant rally information was only disclosed to those scooterists affiliated to the NRC or NSRA who held membership cards accordingly. They would be armed with the dates in question at the beginning of the year, but would only be posted - via a news letter - the information on where to go, two weeks in advance of each rally. A few hiccups occurred in the embryonic stages of this - mainly due to the sheer volume of people involved, but in time it proved to be a successful system. Although many missed the live concerts, and numbers attending fell slightly, the unity of the Scooter Boys, or Scooterists as they started to call themselves, strengthened. The numbers of vans and cars turning up at rallies slowly dwindled, while the scene itself consolidated. Allniters and concerts became the pursuits of weekends between.

The only promoters who did provide entertainment on the runs, was a body called Value For Money Promotions. But like the NRC they provided scooterists' discos only. Without big name bands these wouldn't attract non-scooterists. The main focal point of the rallies returned to being simply the scooter, as again, the Scooter Boy went 'underground'.

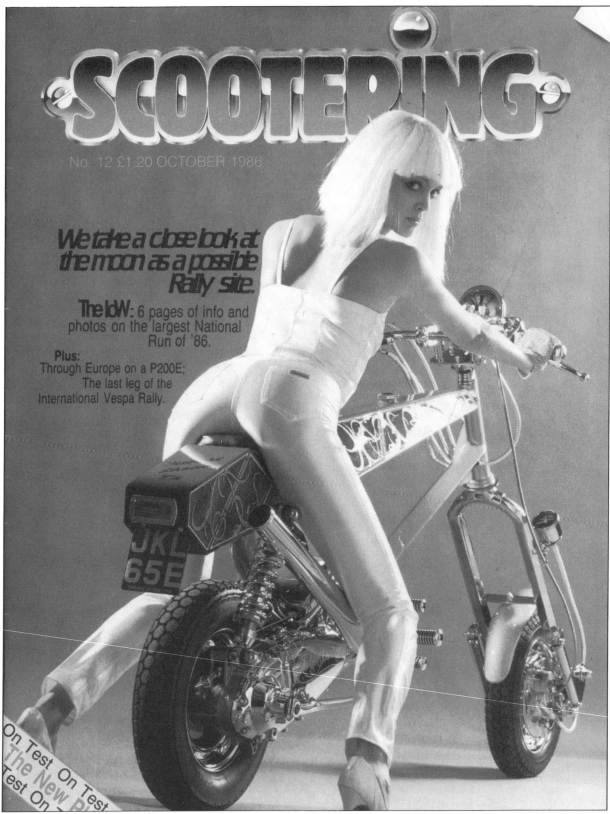

SCOOTERING

No. 12 £1.20 OCTOBER 1986

We take a close look at the moon as a possible Rally site.

The IoW: 6 pages of info and photos on the largest National Run of '86.

Plus:
Through Europe on a P200E;
The last leg of the
International Vespa Rally.

JKL
65E

On Test On Test
The New
Test On

Future Shock — as featured in Scootering Magazine, October 1986

Love Machines

Scooterist's Scooters.

The difference in scooter customising preferences between the Mods and the Scooter Boys, as mentioned in chapter four, took a further step apart in 1983, when Scooter Boys adopted yet another new innovative scooter style - the scooter 'chopper'. The first example of such a machine appeared on the scene around late '82. This prototype, called Futuretta - although an important milestone in customising circles, was anything but aestheticly pleasing.

It wasn't until the Lambretta chopper called Madam Medusa came along in 1983 that an acceptable style for choppers was finally devised. Over the years more and more scooter choppers appeared as their styling grew in popularity. The most memorable of these were the Lambretta-based chops such as Exile (1984), Illusion (1985), Warlord (1987), and New Gold Dream (1988).

The only successful Vespa chopper to gain full recognition, was called Alien, and appeared in 1987. Choppers - usually associated with Bikers - emphasised again the radical differences between Scooter Boys and Mods. They were the following link in the chain of frame sculpting: Modifying scooter frames - mainly by removing bits, was nothing new, and broadly fell in to two categories; skeletons, which had all their panel work removed - including leg shields - and cut-downs, which had their panel work trimmed. These trends had been around since the Sixties, were kept alive by the scooterists of the Seventies, and heavily adopted by the Scooter Boys of the Eighties.

A bastardisation of the chopper and cut-down created a new look for the Vespa around 1984. This style incorporated the slimming of bodywork, and the mounting of a central petrol tank, plus - in some cases - extended forks. The best examples of this style were probably Little Rascal from '83, and Lycanthrope built in late '86.

The Lambretta Chopper Exile, from 1984

The AMS Lambretta/Yamaha YPVS 350 LC

The Vespa Lycanthrope, from 1986

Lambretta oddities with stretched frames like Frustration (1985), and Future Shock (1986) opened another new avenue for customisers, and three-wheeler scooter trikes started appearing towards the end of the Eighties, pushing the boundaries of custom building yet further.

Many of these scooters also featured race-tuned engine kits and performance expansion pipes, which were readily available from a multitude of manufacturers for Vespas and Lambrettas alike. The continuing scooter sport of circuit racing led to road race replicas emerging in the second half of the decade, while full-framed scooters with a high level of cosmetic finish were always prevalent. Intricate engraving, quality painting, and gold and chrome plating often added the final touches for these custom projects, as, to their creators, the hard-earned cash they poured into them - often totalling many thousands of pounds - was considered to be money well spent.

Another way in which scooterists expressed their love for scooters was by renovating rare vintage and classic models back to their original factory specification. This, too, was an expensive and time-consuming trend, and grew in popularity as the Eighties rolled on.

Hybrids and Mongrels

Several scooters fitted with motor-cycle engines were built over the years - some good and some crazy. These were very interesting, created a lot of interest, and demonstrated the customiser's high level of mechanical prowess. But they never really caught on; the only such machine which did gain a certain amount of acceptance was a Lambretta fitted with a Yamaha YPVS 350cc LC engine. This scooter was built by - A&M scooters, for customers - strictly to order.

Custom and classic scooter competitions were always staged at national scooter runs, but the first such exhibition outside the rally scene took place in Nottingham during the autumn of '83. This event was staged by the Notts Britannia scooter club, and set the standards which others were to follow. There after, custom and classic scooter shows were held regularly around the country - with varying degrees of success.

Not all Scooter Boys opted for high-class or original scooters, however. Many were happy enough running around on scooters which were nothing more than clean and tidy, featuring a few bolt-on bits, and a sports exhaust. These were usually T5, or P-range Vespas, the work-horses of the scootering army. Some scooterists, on the other hand, went in a completely different direction. Almost in an act of rebellion against what they perceived as being a false front - based on the fact that many top customs were non-runners and shipped around in vans, they developed the scooter 'rat'. This was the term used to describe deliberately unkempt scoots which more often than not were painted matt black and deliberately kept as dirty as possible - the term 'rat', like the word 'chopper', being borrowed from the biker world - as were many inflences and styles.

A Way Of Life

'The diversity found among the ranks of the Scooter Boy can be directly attributed to the wide ranging appeal, and the cross section of people the name encompassed. Both in music and image, its followers had few limitations, and could pursue their own personal directions. Scootering was - and is - more than an irresponsible interlude of the growing-up process. With its constant resurgence of new blood, it has now become an inter-generational and international movement. It is an all absorbing way of life. To be involved is to understand. To observe is to envy. Now: Enter the Nineties - the Scooter Boys' second decade, with all that it will have to offer'.

Scooter Boys in Europe

One aspect of scootering in the Nineties, is the internationalism hinted at in the closing paragraph of the last section, as by 1990, the British-lead scooter scene had found an array of continental advocates. This has ultimately resulted in much international scooterist interaction, but before this could happen - and before the Federal (Scootering) States of Europe (and beyond) could be established - several British expeditionary forces of Scooter Boys had to make their movement's inaugural incursions into the continent. Having only attended four such forays myself (Versailles, Barcelona, Vienna and Brussels) I'll hand you over Sticky for a full account of how it all happened (**GB**):

'I could never get on with History at school. When it came to explaining why I wanted to give up on the subject I told the teacher that , since I had no plans for the invasion of other European countries, I felt I couldn't really gain anything from the lessons. How wrong I was. Little did I know that in only a few years time I was going to participate in many minor hostile manoeuvres across the channel as a British Scooter Boy on active service. Of course it hadn't always been like that; Fifties scootering was the image of a good mannered pastime, and it wasn't long before scooter clubs from all over Europe were getting together in mass gatherings, for totally peaceful cultural exchanges. The Federation of International Vespa Clubs (FIV) who organised many of these early rallies, are still a strong body. It's EuroVespa events have continued successfully since those halcyon days; along with many other smaller get-togethers, to form a busy calendar for the Vespa enthusiast keen on forging better international relations.

The problem was that something sinister had crawled from the primordial soup of early 80's British youth culture, and it wasn't motivated by forging ties with European brethren. It was motivated by mischief. For those youths who graduated through the 1979 Mod revival into the first Scooter Boys, Europe represented a new challenge.

To them, Europe was seen as a candy store waiting to be raided. This was because it's bars stayed open all night and for the Scooter Boys in search of a party, Holland - with it's red light districts and decriminalised soft drugs - was Nirvana.

The first reconnaissance missions were co-ordinated by Martin Dixon of Scootermania magazine and Nick Jolly of the Ralliest. These took the form of small tours of motorised militia, camping in sites near Amsterdam and Den Haag, and basically behaving like Brits on the piss. These weren't big extravaganzas; generally only thirty or so people, but that was enough for the ferry companies to remember them the following year and refuse to let them travel.

From 1985 onwards, Scooter Boys attendance at the annual EuroVespa rallies - which changed location every year - grew and grew. Both the EuroVespa events of 1985 (Frankfurt) and 1986

(Barcelona) attracted only small British Scooter Boy attendances of less than fifty. By 1987 - and no doubt due to the good press the previous events got in the Scootering press - the Brit attendance for the EuroVespa in Vienna had grown to nearly 250.

The mass invasions continued in1988 with France hosting the EuroVespa at Aix-le-Bains. An infamous arse-bearing incident by a member of the British contingent, at the organised meal being filmed for Italian TV, forever sullied the reputation of the Scooter Boy at EuroVespa. Still, what was abhorrent to the FIV sounded like a bloody good laugh to everyone else, and in 1989, even more British scooterists travelled abroad to sample the fun.

EuroLambretta was another addition to the very busy continental scene in 1989. The first one took place in the French city of Strasbourg, though nobody seemed to know quite why, since it was the Italian Lambretta Club who organised it. This rally passed peacefully enough and was the starting point for several people's scooter tour of the continent, as well as a launch pad for those making their way to that year's EuroVespa rally.

From 1990, the NSRA got in on the act. Their Euro rally that year was to the quiet French town on Saintes, or at least it was quiet till we got there. The image of drunken British Scooter Boys pushing a Union flag draped shopping trolley full of bottles of beer round the sleepy town centre still amused me. Though less than 200 Brits made the effort, the atmosphere here was still one of invasion. It would be quite a few years before international rallies became peaceful affairs again.

European Brethren

Of course the film Quadrophenia - that so influenced the British Mod revival - was also a hit in Europe. Germany, particularly, was heavily influenced by British fashions. With large contingents of British builders and squaddies in some towns and cities, cross-fertilisation was bound to occur. Austria and Belgium, too, had relatively large Mod scenes. All over Europe Lambretta and Vespa riding became a minor fashion again. From Sweden to Spain, lights and mirrors were bolted to scooters, and foxes feared for their tails.

By the mid to late Eighties many of the people in these scenes had metamorphosed into Scooter Boys. The new style of army wear and rally patches in turn attracted whole new generations of fashion conscious youths to roam around the continent in small packs. The role of the new magazines - Scootering and Scooter Scene - can't be underestimated here. Magazines that found their way across to the continent became the GQ of the new Scooter Boys; providing almost up to date fashions in both rally clothing and scooter customising. To their credit, most Europeans didn't out and out copy the British styles, but adapted them to suit their own environments. The Germans for instance, borrowed many fashions from their Biker scene, like the three part top and bottom rocker patch which is used by most of the major German Scooter clubs.

As far as scooters go, European customising has come on in leaps and bounds; again though it is styled to suit the legislation of the country rather than copying the British. Choppers are almost unknown outside the relative legal laxity of the UK, though Stoffi from Austria's groundbreaking chop - Enola Gay - is the exception that proves the rule.

In southern Europe the Mod style of scooter is still preferred. Further north the street racer is the favourite style; with subtle moulding and trimming accompanying loud race-replica paint jobs, thus still remaining legal for road use.

For the landlocked majority though, a seaside scooter rally was only a possibility for the British, or the odd few that ventured over to the UK to check one out.

When European organised rallies did start, they took a form more akin to small inland biker parties than seaside extravaganzas. Someone would find a friendly farmer with some spare land. Ideally it would have a barn or a hall on it, but if not, a marquee would be hired. Disco equipment would then be set up, along with a bar and a food stall, and the host club would run it all.

As with the promoter led UK rallies of the early Eighties, there was money to be made from organising a big rally. Against that, with everyone standing to gain from a good turnout, more entertainment and novelties were included in the price. On the continent the price of entry to a rally usually includes entry to the evening entertainment, and rarely exceeds £10.

As an example, one of the most successful continental rallies is Aachen in Germany; near the Belgium, Dutch border. The organisers are the Filthy Extension SC and the Sly Vultures SC, and they have a reputation for excellent events and gimmicks. If they aren't getting Edwin Starr to perform a set at 3a.m. on Sunday morning, then they are getting aeroplanes to fly over the site pulling banners that read 'welcome scooterists', or giving out free stickers or patches as you come through the gate.

Thanks to more relaxed licensing laws, most continental rallies have allnighters on Friday and Saturday, but the daytime stuck on a field can be rather dull if entertainment isn't provided. As ever, good weather is the best thing for a fine atmosphere, but failing that there are fun-games to watch or take part in. Fun-games might mean light-hearted bungee-running on a slippery tarpaulin, a beer and banana race for scooter riders and pillions, egg catching, pillow fighting or even riding an electric bull. For the more technically inclined there are wheelie competitions or scooter sprints on closed public roads.

If I had to pick a place that symbolised how European rallies should be, it would be Holland. With little indigenous scootering activity, it seems somewhat strange that the country has been host to some of the best scootering events I have ever been on - like the independent German run rally in Groningen in the Eighties, and the EuroLambretta and NSRA rallies at Ockenburgh near Den Haag - but it has. In 1993 the annual Holiday in Holland began; ten days of scootering between two rallies organised by the Anglo-German Speed Demons SC and the Infernal Insects/Scootering Promotions Crew.

All these rallies show how good European scootering could get. They were all peaceful multicultural parties, where freedom of expression wasn't limited by leering bouncers or draconian licensing laws.

Over the years, the scooterists of Europe have got to know each other, with many forming strong friendships that span a whole continent. While patriotic rivalry still plays a part in international proceedings, the early animosity has all but gone. Scooterists from all countries now take each person as they find them, and respect those worthy of respect - wherever they may come from (so long as they truly love and ride their scooters).'

EURO VESPA 87 *Vienna*

The traditional mass migration of mere mortals during the midsummer months to far off shores in search of the sun (a commodity seldom seen in this fair isle), has now become something of a national institution, firmly embedded in the social structure and basic behaviour patterns of twentieth century westernised man.

So when the pre-appointed time of year arrived, I along with nearly 250 other British scooterists conformed to this now socially acceptable practice, but with a subtle difference. The reason behind our foreign travels, was not the prospect of sampling sangria in a Spanish sea-side resort surrounded by señoritas, but to combine it with yet another gut emotion, the driving force behind our daily existence; Scootering.

However, due to mechanical difficulties, I very nearly never made it. As I intended leaving straight from the Rhyl rally on the Sunday, for an 11 o'clock sailing from Felixstowe on the Monday, there was very little leeway for any hiccups whatsoever. Although no one is ever overly pleased to break down, when I sheared all the drive splines on the rear hub of my P200E on the way to Rhyl on the Friday, I considered myself to be quite lucky. Yes that's right, as odd as it may sound, I considered myself to be lucky.

Thanks to my invaluable AA riders club card, it wasn't too long before I found myself complete with ailing scoot outside Morris Braithwaite, a Vespa dealer in Altrincham having my scooter's wrongs put to rights. And I still managed to reach Rhyl in time for an evening session! Thank God the hub didn't last out until the Sunday, when there wouldn't have been a Vespa dealer open, or worse still, you can imagine the dilemma I'd've been in if it hadn't given up the ghost until I was half way across Germany. It doesn't even bare thinking about, does it?

Lead page photograhic montage and copy from Gareth Brown's Vienna Eurovespa rally report as published in issue 23 of SCOOTERING magazine - September 1987.

Who Aren't The New Mods

As stated in the opening pages of this publication, by the mid Nineties, the resurgence of British music - lead scooter culture had become every bit as prolific as it had been during the Mod revivalist days of the late Seventies and early Eighties.

As with the Jam some fifteen years earlier and the Small Faces and The Who some fifteen years before that, these new British bands awoke million of their followers to the Modernist facet of the on-going culture that is scootering. Although these fans didn't all then rush out and buy a scooter, the aforementioned endorsements helped swell the ranks of the tangentially developing "New Mod" movement dramatically.

Unable to be jointly categorised as Mods though - and in true tabloid tradition - these bands became generally pigeon holed together under the banner of 'Britpop' courtesy of a most confused press. Mark Taylor now tells the tale (**GB**):

The Birth of Britpop and the faceless generation

Britpop - and to an extent 'New Modernism' - began life as a throwaway term used by lazy music journalists to cover a motley collection of guitar-driven groups that they were otherwise unable to label in the summer of 1994.

The sound, meaning, background and talent of the bands lumped under the Britpop umbrella varied so much though, that within months of its creation, it had become an irritating albatross around the necks of all it tarnished.

The only common link between the 'Britpop' groups was the simple fact that they were British, guitar-led and had no identifiable image of tag attached to them.

While the media were having trouble labelling this music however, they had even bigger problems with the vast audiences buying the records and attending the gigs. For unlike previous musical generations, this one was faceless with no readily identifiable style of youth cult attached to it. Just as it had been with house music before, it was the music that would provide the key.

The influence of house and clubbing on all music since the late 1980's and the 'summers of love' cannot be underestimated. In a similar way to punk's cleansing of the 1970's, it had shown people and musicians in particular, that there was no need to be pigeon-holed and that there was certainly no problem with borrowing and celebrating ideas and influences from the past.

At the apex of this non-existent new 'movement' were two bands who in the course of two summers were to propel British music back onto centre stage simply by virtue of being just that - British - and not a pale imitation of all things American as had dominated proceedings this side of the Atlantic for much of the previous 15 years.

The names of these two musical messiahs were Blur and Oasis, who in addition to hailing from opposite ends of the country and social spectrums, were at equally different stages in their own musical heritage.

Blur, a quartet from deepest Essex, had first risen to prominence in 1991 when they hit the charts with the single 'There's No Other Way', taken off their debut album 'Leisure'. A period of commercial and artistic regrouping around the heavily mod-influenced second album 'Modern Life is Rubbish', saw them bounce back to the top of the tree in 1994 with their ubiquitous all-conquering tribute to all-things English: 'Parklife'.

With its chatalong chirpiness, varied structure and singer Damon Albarn's self-effacing 'mockernee' accent this single not only deserved all it's plaudits and massive sales, but also welcomed the comparisons to that earlier uncompromising and equally indefinable English Mod musical maestro: Ray Davies of The Kinks.

It was through these comparisons of Blur - together with their classic English imagery, guitarist Graham's taste for Mod fashion and even accusations of London image-mongering - that the tag of 'new Mods' was suddenly being bandid about for the first time since 'Secret Affair', and fellow Essex boys 'The Purple Hearts' had called it a day in the early 1980's.

In 1995, Blur received across the board Brit award success, gave a sell-out cockney knees-up gig in London's Mile End and had their first number one single with 'Country House'. Their subsequent album 'The Great Escape' however, proved a leap too far and lost them much middle England support to the band Oasis, who by them were more than ready to take a well deserved musical and cultural lead in the Britpop/New Mod scene and beyond.

Oasis - a lively Mancunian fivepiece based around the combined forces of singer-frontman Liam Gallagher and the quality songmanship of elder brother Noel - followed their earlier promise and grabbed 'middle England' middle-ground for themselves.

Formed initially by Liam, but hijacked by the talent of Noel Gallagher, Oasis grabbed much attention when they blasted their way onto Alan McGhee's ground breaking Creation record label in 1993.

Early releases and performance had hinted at what was to come but it was the genius of, first 'Live Forever' and later 'Whatever' (which reached number three in the charts at Christmas 1994) that really marked their mainstream arrival.

From there on, the only way for Oasis was up, as they took on and beat allcomers with a series of first class tracks (Wonderwall, Morning Glory, Don't Look Back in Anger et al) that provided everything - including a unique image.

Oasis's style owed more to their Manchester roots and the late 80s imagery of "Madchester's" baggiedom (as popularised by the likes of friends and mentors Happy Mondays, Stone Roses

(Top left) Steve Craddock of OCS with his Lambretta Li150 Series II and girlfriend 'H'.
(Top right) Ocean Colour Scene.

All five Oasis band members on their Italijet scooters outside of Earls Court in
London - 1995.

and Inspiral Carpets) than traditional Modernism. In fact, Noel had actually been both a roadie and rejected singer with the Carpets, in what he has later described as a "great learning experience".

National newspaper pictures of all five Oasis band members on scooters at Earls Court did see them strongly linked to previous eras however, as did Noel's oft-working with the two Pauls; McCartney and Weller.

Paul Weller had always been 'targeted' with all things Mod from his days with The Jam, but after his ridiculously hasty sacking by Polydor at the tail end of the 1980's, many had wondered whether he would have the appetite to rise again. But rise he did though and as his career accelerated through a series of award and critic conquering solo albums in the mid 1990's, he found himself honoured with the monicker of "Modfather".

Regular live and recorded tie-ups with fellow scooter rider Noel Gallagher aided both the image and the quality of Paul's products, as did working with rising Birmingham band Ocean Colour Scene. OCS, led by singer Simon Fowler and guitarist Steve Craddock, had gained prominence in those earlier baggy days, but due to a variety of record company hassles, had been forced into a lengthy sabbatical.

A fellow lover of the scooter, guitarist Steve Craddock (and bass player Damon Minchella) of OCS first teamed up with Paul Weller for his 'Wild Wood' album and followed this with appearances on 'Stanley Road' and numerous tours at home and away.

With both Weller and Oasis dropping the OCS name into conversation and interviews left, right and centre, the time was suddenly ripe for Ocean Colour Scene themselves to return and in early 1996, first 'The Riverboat Song' and then 'You've Got It Bad' fired into the charts, while their new album 'Moseley Shoals' was unleashed to critical acclaim, and reached number two in the album charts in April of the same year.

Fellow members of this "scene with no name" make equally impressive reading and all are just as hard to label.

Coming in from the sidelines after nearly ten years of trying were Pulp, led by the angular mis-shaped popularity and genius of Michael Jackson baiter Jarvis Cocker, while from the depths of the Mersey came the well-placed rise of brilliant Liverpudlian janglers Cast - fronted by former Las man John Power.

The feminine side has been represented by the punk-edged pop swords of Elastica and Sleeper, while youth finds itself with no shortage of talent among the next generation, with the sideburn-swiped fun of Supergrass being ably supported by the fashion-conscious posturing of Menswear, the teenage attitude of Northern Uproar and the pop niceties of The Bluetones.

There you have it - a scene so ridiculously varied as to make all categorising labels redundant - particularly one as trite and bubble gum as Britpop.

For just as the scooterists had rejected main stream fashion as impractical and irrelevant in the mid-Eighties, so on a far larger scale, their musical counterparts were doing the same some ten years later.

. . .So that's the story Morning Glory and an insight into a compelling 'Way of Life'. To be involved is to understand. To observe is to envy. Now enter the 21st Century and all it has to offer. . . (Gareth Brown).

Bibliography

'Mods'   **by Richard Barnes**
    1989 Plexus Publishing ltd   ISBN 0 906008 14X

'You'll Never Be Sixteen Again'   **by Peter Everett**
    1986 BBC Publications   ISBN 0563 205334

'The Teds'   **by Chris Steel-Perkins and Richard Smith**
    1979 Travelling Light/Exit   ISBN 906333 059

'Bikers'   **by Dr Maz Harris**
    1985 Faber and Faber   ISBN 0 571 13510 2

'Rockers'   **by Johnny Stuart**
    1987 Plexus Publishing ltd   ISBN 0 85965 125 8

'Cafe Racers'   **by Mike Clay**
    1988 Osprey Publishing ltd   ISBN 0 85045 677 0

'Motor Scooters'   **by Michael Webster**
    1986 Shire Publications ltd   ISBN 0 85263 836 1

'The Scooter'   **by Jon Stevens**
    1972 Constable and Co ltd   ISBN 0 09458 790 6

'Sweet Soul Music'   **by Peter Goralnick**
    1986 Virgin Books   ISBN 0 86369 135 8

'British Beat Groups of the Sixties' **by Colin Cross, Paul Kendall, and Mick Farren**
    1980 Omnibus Press   ISBN 86001 638 2

'Quadrophenia'   **by Alan Fletcher**
    1979 Corgi Books/Eel Pie   ISBN 0 0552 111 83X